OUR LAST SUMMER

A PERSONAL MEMOIR

OUR LAST SUMMER

Ajay Peter Manuel

iUniverse LLC
Bloomington

OUR LAST SUMMER
A PERSONAL MEMOIR

iUniverse books may be ordered through booksellers or by contacting:

iUniverse
1663 Liberty Drive
Bloomington, IN 47403
www.iuniverse.com
1-800-Authors (1-800-288-4677)

ISBN: 978-1-4759-9573-2 (sc)
ISBN: 978-1-4759-9575-6 (hc)
ISBN: 978-1-4759-9574-9 (e)

Library of Congress Control Number: 2013911430

Printed in the United States of America.

iUniverse rev. date: 8/23/13

To my love for you, Mom and Dad.
To the support of my friends,
And to the inspiration and faith
Of one young girl who will always be my world—
Annie,
If not for you,
This book wouldn't be.

CONTENTS

PREFACE

A great man once said, "Let not the passing clouds trouble you. The sky is clearer if you calmly look at it with your eyes wide open. You have then started your journey. There will always be ups and downs. Otherwise, life won't be exciting. But at the same time, when you keep thinking and dreaming about your destination, your journey and resolve will get stronger."

That man was my father, and he was right.

There is a time in everyone's life when we are confronted by an experience that is beyond our comprehension. It happened to me when I first fell in love. Love helped me understand the truth about several things in life, including myself.

It felt as if I was on a journey in pursuit of a destination that I was yet to discover. But after a while, love also taught me that sometimes in life, the journey is the destination. My journey had truly begun in my childhood. My naïveté restricted my comprehension of this reality.

Now I know that I am where I am—and who I am—because of the love of three people who mean the world to me: my father, mother, and sister. In their company, I learned the importance of being able to love and to be willing to share it with others. In my father's shadow, I learned to be courageous; in my mother's comfort, I found strength. In my younger sister's happiness, I found mine.

I became a healthy, optimistic, and determined young man. I loved my family, and I lived every day of my life for them. More importantly, I also learned to live with true freedom. If I had to compare my journey to a voyage at sea, I would be the man who sailed the seas with utmost passion and independence. And when I first fell in love, I learned an even greater lesson.

I realized that to live free, one should be willing to accept all that comes along in life. Be it success, joy, failure, or disappointment, a man who lives freely should be able to accept the reality of such experiences; even when all is lost, continue to live with hope and dream to strive for the best.

These lessons were of great personal value, and yet they were the results of the simplest experiences and events of my life—as simple as falling in love with a girl. If one is willing to observe, feel, and accept even the most ordinary and difficult circumstances with a full heart, life will bring beautiful experiences.

I'm willing to share my experiences with you. It is a wonderful story; my roller coaster of emotions involves love, friendships, betrayals, misgivings, and life. My motto is: *Cherish the past, live the present, and anticipate the future.*

For now, I would like to take this chance to revisit these memories one last time with you in *Our Last Summer.*

INTRODUCTION

It has been three years since I last visited Khartoum, Sudan. Life changed dramatically after my departure to Edmonton, Canada. I left at the end of August 2009 to pursue higher studies at the University of Alberta. My last visit to Sudan was during the annual summer break of 2010. After that, my family was transferred to a different country, courtesy of my dad's employment in the organization PLAN International, similar to the humanitarian aid/relief agencies such as UNICEF and CARE. His five-year contract in Sudan had reached an end, and he was relocated to another branch in Sierra Leone.

I've lived in Africa since our family's first transfer from our hometown in Madurai, India, to Egypt. This goes back as far as the year 2001. I was a ten-year-old kid at that point. My first four years in Cairo were difficult. I was enrolled in Cairo American College (CAC).

Although I was able to successfully complete my elementary and middle school education at CAC, it was a harsh experience from the beginning. I endured racism and social segregation in the student community; in the end, I was thankful to be accepted by a special set of friends.

I didn't cherish my memories in Egypt and expected no difference when we were transferred to Sudan. I enrolled at the Khartoum American School (KAS). Over the years, I was proven wrong. I graduated from high school in the summer of 2009. By then, I identified Sudan as my second home. My memories at KAS were beautiful. My life—and my journey toward becoming a mature teenager—began in Sudan.

My personality and my outlook on life changed gradually during high school. My circle of friends grew even larger. I would engage with several personalities, many of whom I now consider my best friends. I never expected that our days together would be so short. After graduation, we took our own respective paths in life, once again becoming acquaintances in time's passing. Nevertheless, our memories remain. Through my experiences in Sudan, I also learned to accept and forego my initial attitudes about my life in Egypt. This gave me the opportunity to get back in touch with my friends at CAC.

I completed my final year of undergraduate studies (September 2012–May 2013) at the University of Alberta, and have graduated with a BSc. (Honors) Astrophysics degree. My life has changed dramatically in the span of a few years. There are still a lot of decisions to be made for the future, but I've decided to go with the flow and let life come to me.

I hope to return to Sudan in the near future. This book is a dedication to the memories and life I had in Sudan. Time is an endless pursuit, passing us at every turn; sometimes it causes the fine line between a past memory and reality to be ambiguous. I can take comfort in justifying my feelings about my memories by writing passionately about them and knowing that there were others who experienced the same with me.

CHAPTER 1

GRADUATION

"In life, there are no ends, only new beginnings."

The silence permeating the atmosphere within the small gathering of figures in black coats and hats surrounding the garden compound gave way to a sudden tremor of raucous ovation that lit the night sky.

A person in the crowd could easily identify the contrasting colors of the scenario. The bright stage, lighting around the garden, and flashing cameras were overshadowed by the friendly commotion of graduation caps flung in the air as students and friends embraced one another in joy. It was graduation night for the class of 2009.

The happiness that sustained the emotions felt within that short instance of laughter and applause was accompanied by tears; tears flowed as I embraced my dear friend Cindy and whispered my well wishes for her future. We would now begin our selective journeys in life. This would be our last night together.

The crowd slowly dissipated toward the main quad; a grand buffet had been arranged a few feet away from the garden. The quad was a wide, concrete assembly formally used for school announcements. Tonight, it served to entertain the students, professors, and families. Life passed by in a glance that night. I enjoyed each and every moment, and I indulged myself in the freshness of it all: the family pictures, the melancholic and somber farewells, and the delicious graduation cake.

Wherever I turned, I was greeted by well wishes for my future.

I felt at home with my company that night. I anticipated a bright and adventurous future, but my heart was still laden with emotions suppressed deep within me. I was disappointed by how a memorable part of my life—that I had wanted to last forever—had found its course all too soon.

I was spent emotionally when I returned home from the prom at one o'clock in the morning. The streets were empty but familiar. A few lampposts lit up the street corners. I favored walking in the darkness. It gave me a sense of closure from the outside world, allowing me to balance the emotional tides in my heart. After moments of random wanderings, I finally made it back to my apartment complex. My family and I lived in an apartment on the third floor. The expansive complex had a swimming pool near the gates that also enclosed the parking spaces.

I had informed my family earlier about the prom. I knew that Mom and Dad would be exhausted after the long day, but when I entered the apartment, I had a preemptive notion that they were still awake—and awaiting my arrival. They would always wait to bid me good night, no matter how long it took or how late it was. They loved me so much.

Our apartment complex was about fifteen minutes away from KAS. The prom had taken place at a nearby location, making my walk home a suitable distance. From our kitchen, we could see directly across to the airport. The opposite streets were lined with restaurants that remained open for the night.

The apartment opened to a wide veranda filled with couches, showcases of ceramic figurines, art tapestries, and a large TV that could be seen across from the entrance. To the left, a series of pillars and corridors separated the kitchen and the dining table. There were three bedrooms. My parents used the master bedroom in the far right corner of the apartment. Annie and I occupied the bedrooms at the opposite end of the apartment.

Slipping off my shoes quietly, I made my way down to Annie's room. I saw a light shining through the crevices of the door and knew she might be up reading a book as usual. Without the knowledge of our parents, she would use any opportunity to pull me to her room so we could read books together or talk the night away until she fell asleep on my shoulder. This would finally allow me to tuck her in and then pursue the sleep that I needed.

With the occasional creaking of the door, I slowly nudged my head around the corner to find Annie, surprisingly, fast asleep under the blanket. Her copy of *The Berenstain Bears* was tucked under her arms. Her small, round face poked out from the corners of the blanket. With her rosy complexion, she appeared cute and angelic. In reality, she was an exemplary model of Loki, the Norse god of mischief.

She had wept sincerely throughout the graduation ceremony. It finally dawned on her that I would now be absent from school, and she would miss my company. After receiving my diploma, I had teased her about crying. Shunning my remarks, she had given me a warm hug, a kiss on the cheek, and had whispered, "I love you" in my ear. Although she often enjoyed getting me in trouble, her actions tonight showed that she still loved her older brother.

Being careful not to wake her up, I gently tugged the book from under her arms, lightly stroked her cheeks, and gave her a small kiss on the forehead. She was fast asleep. After tucking her in and turning down the lamp, I proceeded to my parents' room.

In the hallway, I paused briefly at Grandpa Antony's (Mom's father) portrait. Six years had passed since his death. I loved him greatly. He had been a wonderful mentor. His death came as a shock to all of us, and I was distraught the day we received the sad news. I was certain that he had been there in the crowd with my family tonight, cheering me on, and wishing well for my future. The thought made me smile.

As I approached my parents' room, I heard their conversing voices. I stepped in to find them relaxing on the bed. The lights were on, and their faces brightened as they saw me approach. Giving them both hugs, I got down on my knees and received their blessings. This was a customary gesture in our culture, in respect of our elders. I considered my family to be my world. Due to weak and strained relations, our family was perceived as outcasts, isolated from our relatives. Consequently, my family and I were dependent upon each other at some level. I had great respect for my parents, and I loved them dearly.

Dad was like my best friend. A great man in all his actions, I wished to emulate him in life. Besides Mom and Annie, he was the one other person I could talk to about anything. Dad's dreamy personality was balanced by Mom's practicality; together, they were my best counsel.

We were still surprised by how the years had passed before this momentous occasion. Under financial distress, Dad worked hard in his younger years, when we were in India, to support the family. Considering this, he shared only a few memories of my childhood. He never had the chance to see me grow up; ergo he was shocked that I had already graduated from school. Mom, meanwhile, had been a constant companion. She held me close all my life; beneath her stern attitudes, she had great love. She was the heart of our family.

Late as it was, I quickly delved into the details of the prom. A few minutes later, I was kicked out of the room to get some well-deserved sleep after a great year of success and achievement. I couldn't fall asleep very easily. In bed, I recollected the memories of my journey through high school. I finally dozed off after a few hours of being immersed in contentious feelings.

I spent the following day as a lazy bilge rat, starving from the physical and mental fatigue I had accumulated over the year. Dad was to attend a meeting in Malawi. He was the sponsorship and grants manager at PLAN International. After much persuasion, I assisted him in packing and his subsequent departure.

Dad and I were comic relief for our family. In his absence, the week dragged on and was filled with boredom. Because of my busy, selfish focus on academics and social life at school, I had lost several opportunities to bond with my family. Now that I had graduated, I wanted to spend quality time with my parents and enjoy this period of respite.

To keep busy, I spent the week packing away the gigantic collection of folders, binders, and notebooks I had accumulated during high school. It was an extensive renovation of my room, and the mess was unbelievable. It amused me that I had retained notes and papers since ninth grade. As tiresome as it was, I found great joy in the effort.

Browsing through my folders, I was struck by a bout of nostalgia. This made it even more difficult to throw away what I found, ranging from scrap sketches to random paper conversations. It represented a vast portion of my high school memories. In the end, it took the combined efforts of Mom and Annie to persuade me to actually clean my room rather than organize a secondary memory storage plan.

We had lived in Sudan for four years. Dad's work was beneficial to the family; it provided the opportunity for an international education for Annie and me. Simultaneously, our constant transfers from one country to another meant we never had a permanent home. I did not have friends on a daily basis, but I couldn't deny the strong feeling of home that I identified with my memories and life in Sudan. This may be due to my experiences as a maturing teenager over my years at KAS.

Dad's contract in Sudan was initially supposed to last until my graduation. We were given the option of extending the contract for an extra year—thanks to Dad's extraordinary work ethic and achievements in his organization. We greeted him on his return from Malawi the following week. As usual, we couldn't conceal our excitement for the souvenirs and gifts he had brought from his trip. Dad's return trips were always enjoyable. Dad would endorse his role as a *griot* (an African storyteller) while relating his adventures abroad. Mom, Annie, and I were an eager audience.

His return also foreshadowed the necessity for a discussion

regarding the family's future. I had an invitation to a get-together with my friends one evening, and I couldn't hide my grumpy attitude toward my parents. My mood was partially ruined because of a heated discussion with them earlier that evening about my plans for university.

I had expressed my desire to study abroad, particularly in Canada. With my performance in high school and my outstanding academic profile, my professors believed I could easily secure admission to the highest-ranked universities. The one major obstacle in our way was money.

Dad had toiled and worked hard for the happiness of our family for more than twenty years. His reason for working with PLAN stemmed from his personal attitudes toward helping communities— and his desire to provide his children with the benefits of a good education and upbringing. Dad had incurred financial challenges in order for us to have secure lives with wonderful benefits in Egypt and Sudan. Furthermore, as time passed by, there were clear signs of his aging—physically, mentally, and spiritually.

His work had gradually developed into a burden that he carried for the sake of his family. It didn't help when he lost his best friends. They were jealous of his success, and they only cared about his friendship in the context of his financial status. Slowly but surely, he also began to lose his vigor and interest in his job; it started exercising ignorant politics above moral attitudes. He even confessed once that he was at a loss toward his sense of identity and happiness.

If I were to opt for my higher studies abroad, it would only mean that he would have to continue his work in PLAN—and his burdensome life. I felt guilty and depressed by this thought.

My desire was to prove to my parents that I could find my own place, cultivate my own life, and support the family so that Mom and Dad could settle down peacefully. I dreamed of a day when I could return home, welcomed by the happiness in their eyes and the overwhelming love and warmth of my family's presence. My eagerness to reach higher grounds and goals could only be accomplished if I studied in Canada. During the party, I was lost in speculation about what to do, and my failure to support my parents.

When I returned home that night, I realized it was all about a choice that had to be made. This one choice had the potential to change my life. Confused, I made a wish that something would happen in the near future to help with my decision. The wish came true faster than I expected.

After a few days, I received the results of my application to the University of Alberta. To my surprise, I had secured several scholarships and awards granting me a total of $64,000 in financial aid. The amount was incredible, and it was enough to seal my years in Canada. The awards were divided over the four years of my academic program. I would be required to partake in on- and off-campus employment to garner further income and financial assistance.

Even with the good news, a large sum of money was still required from my parents to support my education at the University of Alberta. Upon hearing the results, Dad congratulated me on my achievements, noting that my hard work in high school had paid off. When I asked if I could go to Canada, he smiled and said, "I'll think about it."

With that reaction, I had a good hunch I had secured my dream of studying in Canada. A certain degree of guilt remained in my heart about the decision, and I knew I wanted to share this with him. I just had to find the opportune moment to do so. It happened one night when Dad and I took a stroll to get food at a nearby restaurant.

When he brought up the topic, I was surprised that he already knew my feelings. It made it a lot easier for me, and I was glad to share my thoughts about all the changes occurring in my life. Minutes seemed like hours, but Dad was firm and strong with his decision.

He said, "Son, I live my life for you, and I'm very proud of you.

But don't ever feel guilty for what you have now. I know the pain that I felt at your age when I didn't have the needs to sustain and fuel my dreams. If I had, I would have a different life. But, now, even if I were offered the chance to live my life over, I wouldn't change one bit of it. You know why? 'Cause I found three beautiful stars that guide me, keep me warm, and love me for all they have: you, Mom, and Annie. I'm so proud of you for sharing this with me, but as your father, I believe in my responsibility to provide you the best I can so that, one day, you can do the same for one who may follow your side. I'm happy with the choice I have made to send you to Canada for your higher studies. I know it will be difficult, but with the support, love, and compassion that I get from the three of you, nothing in life seems impossible to me. I want to see you accomplish your dreams, and reach for the skies."

"But, Dad—"

"No buts. If you feel you owe me something, I ask for one favor. Do your best, live your life the way you want to, reach your goals, establish your future, and—most importantly—take care of your family and love them for all you have. Will you do that for me?"

Those words melted away my fears. Where there had been doubt, there was conviction. I now had a purpose and a future to look forward to. I replied, "I will, Dad. That's a promise."

"Good! Now let's go get our food because I'm hungry—and I know your mom is going to kill me if we are late!"

It only struck me then that Dad had intentionally walked us past the restaurant several times during our conversation so he could give me his undivided attention. I had been so immersed in our conversation that I had failed to recognize this.

Only a week remained until we were to head back to Madurai to meet Grandma Mary. My grandparents from Dad's side of the family had passed away before my birth. Grandma Mary was our immediate relation from Mom's side of the family. She moved into our house in Madurai after Grandpa Antony's death.

Approaching the date of our departure, I felt I needed to make up for my glum appearance at my friends' party earlier on. My family had yet to decide if I would go to Canada directly from India or if I would be returning to Sudan beforehand. Given this scenario, my friends and I presumed that this was our final gathering, and we arranged a farewell. It consisted of a small group of my closest friends who were still in Sudan. The same host of our previous get-together accommodated my farewell. This time, rather than being secluded in my thoughts, I enjoyed each and every moment of the party.

I took as many pictures as possible to sustain my final memories with my friends. Even if I were to return to Sudan before my departure to Canada, I would not be seeing most of my friends since they would depart during my absence. Lunch was self-provided. We said, "Let's cook ourselves some grub." Although there was a faint sense of disappointment in my departure, I was certain I would cross paths with many of my friends in the near future.

A few days later, I found myself seated on the seven-hour flight to Madurai. Relaxing my head on the windowpane, I looked out to the sky and began thinking about the last four years of my life at KAS. Eleventh grade, in particular, had been an exhilarating ride. There were several losses and surprises; I hadn't thought it possible to recover from the emotional injuries and entanglements I encountered that year. Somehow I had made it. I still remembered the wish.

Before the start of twelfth grade, I wished that my final year at KAS would simply be better and that I would find a means to overcome my difficulties in eleventh grade and obtain a source of happiness. It felt childish at that moment. I believed then that I had made the wish as a lie for my own comfort. After all that happened, I had clearly been wrong.

What I believed to be a lie became a reality. This reality lasted a year but seemed like an eternity—a reality I would like to share, and only understood as I moved on.

The days have gone and passed us by,
But our memories together will remain alive.
Our time has come to a momentary end;
Our new adventure is yet to begin.
A journey that is inconceivable,
But an expedition we believe is not impossible.
Standing here, I look at the past.
To my side, remains the future, and I feel lost.
Lost in speculation, lost in thought,
I feel numb inside; hard to believe that time has just flown by.
Tears slide down my cheeks,
And I cry, not sad, but happy at our remembrances together.
Life is where I am going.
The past is to be loved, the present to be lived, and the future to be
*   anticipated.*
Stepping toward the unknown,
It feels that being together we might not be alone.
Grief shared, tears wept, moments spent,
We realize that it is finally time to move on.

It was the beginning of my memories of our last summer.

CHAPTER 2

FIRST ACQUAINTANCE

"When you're flirting with a girl, choose your words wisely."

"I hate you."

Those three words summed up her first impression of me. Three words that guys, in general, just don't like to hear from a girl—three words that make any guy sulk. They certainly made me feel that way. Never in my wildest dreams could I have imagined that these words would mark the beginning of a wonderful friendship.

Our first acquaintance was at an interschool debating council. I was in eleventh grade at that point, and we were nearing the end of the school year. Khartoum International Community School (KICS) was one of the few internationally accredited educational institutions in Sudan besides KAS. The schools shared a friendly rivalry in significant educational promotions and recreational sports tournaments that were organized on an annual basis.

The prior year, the schools began hosting inter-school debates for Model United Nations (MUN), an academic simulation of the United Nations. Participants usually role-play as diplomats representing a particular nation or NGO in a simulated conference of the United Nations, including the Security Council or the General Assembly. Sessions involved critical discussions of solutions and developments on international issues.

In my viewpoint, MUN didn't present an explicit sense of competition. It was an opportunity for students from both academic communities to share and criticize global ideas and opinions. My interest and talent in oration secured my leadership as the president of the KAS MUN council. It was my first experience as a member, and I couldn't hold back my excitement in silencing the KICS delegation hosting the conference. The weekend conference started late on a Thursday. Thursday night was an opening ceremony of sorts; representatives of both delegations gave introductory speeches, and there was an informal mixer/dinner. It was like the calm before a storm. The debates would begin the following day.

A boardroom was chosen for our sessions. Discussions focused on the Darfur crisis in Southern Sudan. Since my arrival in Sudan, I had learned about the divisions between the communities of the Northern and Southern Sudanese peoples. These divisions delved into religious and ethnic differences, with a Muslim-dominated North and a Christian-dominated South. Political differences and further friction had incited a longstanding strife between the two sides, resulting in the North's marginalization of the South's resources and culminating in the Darfur crisis.

Student members of both schools representing different nations around the world were to "diplomatically" argue their views on the impending crisis and negotiate a general resolution. As president of the KAS team, I was given the responsibility of leading and supporting my peers during the sessions. In order to communicate with other representatives, written paper notes were passed around the tables during the debate. That's when she came into the story.

She was a chauffeur among several others who served to pass out necessary documentations and papers between team members. Our argument hinged on the fact that she had misplaced one of my notes and mistakenly offered it to the opposing team. I'm usually patient and calm under any situation, and I knew it was an accident. But as always, I gave in to my yearning to tease my peers and friends. I decided to use this situation as a justification to meticulously tease her after the session ended for lunch.

A buffet was arranged in the student lounge. I caught up with her near the coffee table and introduced myself. After a while, I slowly began implicating her about her actions earlier. I kept a stern attitude, but I was hoping she would realize I was just playing a prank on her. That line of thought didn't exactly work out.

"By the way, weren't you the one who misplaced my notes during the debate?" I asked while trying to be serious.

Her reply couldn't have been any slower. "Uh. Yes. I was hoping you would have avoided remembering that. But I'm so sorry. I didn't mean to do it. This is actually my first time. I—"

"Be it your first time or last, just don't make any more mistakes. You pretty much passed out the information we were going to use to hit the opposition. Of course, it didn't work out. Anyways, excuse me, I need to get myself a cup of coffee," I replied, completely cutting her off and walking away.

The plan had initially been for me to get a cup of coffee for her and then let her in on the prank. But, as I walked away, replaying what I had said in my mind, I realized that my prank hadn't come across too well. I felt as if I had just incriminated an innocent person. Stopping in my tracks, I turned around immediately to apologize and let her in on the truth, but she was nowhere to be seen. It didn't take me long to identify the distraught figure moving through the crowd and out of the lounge. I couldn't help but accept the flashing signs in my mind. *Crap!*

I rushed after her, muttering about how stupid I was. To make matters worse, I didn't even know her name. I ran and shouted, "Hey, girl! Wait up!" I caught up to her by the boardroom. She was not pleased to see me again. I suppose that was inevitable. Not wasting any time, I quickly said, "I'm sorry I was only—"

That was all I could get out. Usually, I can assert myself in any argument—and even an apology. I couldn't believe it. She totally threw me off! It was a tough lesson.

She said, "I hate you!" Three words—and she might as well have killed me then. Having said this, she continued to walk away, distress and frustration etched on her face. I have to confess, I can maintain a firm attitude toward other guys when the situation calls for it, but it only takes one pretty girl passing my way to make me soft. Now I had one pretty girl pretty close to tears all because of me. I felt very guilty.

I believe that everyone deserves a second chance—no matter what mistakes they have made. I say that inclusively. I felt I needed a second chance in this situation. That belief became a strong emotion as the debate concluded that evening. I got my second chance once the meeting ended and the participants began to disperse.

As the chauffeur, she had to stay behind and clean up around the conference hall. I was proficient enough in making imaginary scenarios to ward off my team so I could find some space to talk with her. I edged in silently. She was trying to move one of the tables to the outer edge of the room. From where I was standing, I could see she was having a difficult time with the job.

I said, "May I offer you a hand?" Six words, first mistake.

It took her a second to recall my face and figure. Ignoring me, she continued her struggle. But I persisted.

"You know, I can pick that up for you."

"No, it's okay. Please let me just finish—"

"No, no. I can do this," I interrupted and swiftly picked up the table. Second mistake.

I repeated a mantra—*Yeah, you can do this*—in my mind for the next few minutes as I carried the table to the other side of the conference hall. It was really heavy. Either that or I was weak as ever. I went with the former choice. Eventually, we began talking. I was able to apologize for my earlier actions, and soon we were engaged in a lively conversation. An hour passed by before it was time for us to leave. Since we attended different schools, I knew that it would be rare for us to meet again. We exchanged e-mail addresses; I hoped we could keep in touch.

Before driving off that evening, I realized I had forgotten to ask her name.

"Hey! This is ridiculous, but I totally forgot to ask. What's your name?"

"Tina."

That was it for our acquaintance. I didn't foresee that she would become one of my closest friends in the near future. I will never forget our memories together.

I successfully completed eleventh grade that year. At that point, my life was a gong show. I was a living role model of the movie *Titanic*—with the exception of the love and happy parts. I was under a lot of stress, confusion, and pressure. Earlier that year, my social life had become a struggle for love and attention, or, more fittingly, an infatuation. It was all for a girl I became friends with during frequent meetings at the school library. Her name was Rigel.

Rigel and I shared the same schedule and spent our free block periods, involving independent studies, at the library. Through our interactions, I learned more about her. It didn't take long before I realized that I had begun to like her unconsciously. That was when my life took a turn for the better—or the worse. Now when I think back to those moments, I ask myself, *"What the heck was that all about?"* or even *"Are you kidding yourself?"*

Two of my friends at school, Kevin and Mark, were also close friends of Rigel. They were aware that I had fallen head over heels for her. It took three months before I actually had the nerve to ask her out. I couldn't deny my nervousness; it was one of the few instances where I actually liked a girl to a great extent. The result was a catastrophe. I still remember how it went down. How can I forget it? I was handed the noose that day.

Lunch was served at the outdoor cafeteria under a hearth of trees, across from the quad and next to the science laboratory. One might wonder how we ever survived the heat of the country when temperatures rose to 45 degrees Celsius by noon. But thanks to a friendly crowd of natural vegetation, gardens, and grass playgrounds, we were welcomed by cool winds that satiated the occupants of the cafeteria. The basketball courts were set in between the small field used by the elementary and middle school kids and the larger track and field on the other side of the courts.

A turtle enclosure was located behind the cafeteria under the shade of a few trees. I chose that as my location. It took some time, but I was able to catch Rigel's attention as she conversed with her friends. Leading her to the enclosure, we sat down together. With Kevin and Mark watching from afar, I confessed to Rigel how I truly felt about her.

"Rigel, I haven't known you for a long time. In fact, it's only been during our interactions at the library the past few months that we became good friends. I don't know what it might mean to you, but I believe that I've started yearning more for your company and friendship. I feel it would be great if we could be closer to each other and get to know each other on a personal basis. Simply, I was wondering if you would accept my offer to go out with me. Not as a friend. I suppose you already understand where I'm going with this."

That was it? I wanted to hit my head on a wall. After countless days of rehearsing what I wanted to say and the countless scenarios I had envisioned, I couldn't believe this was all I could come up with. *What happened to my swag?*

Rigel took her time to reply. Her hesitation was obvious as she tried to put thoughts together with words. In the end, she said, "I've always liked you. I've enjoyed my time in your company." I could clearly hear the voice in my mind saying, *Well, well, we're getting somewhere.* I felt as if things were playing to my side. But with those words, she followed up with a wonderful statement every guy who likes a girl dreads to hear. "But I only see you as a friend. I hope I haven't hurt you. I know this may not be what you wanted to hear, but frankly, you're not the type of guy I'm looking for." In short, I had just been friend-zoned.

I didn't know what she had been thinking or feeling when she said those words, but their effect was potentially devastating to me. Weirdly enough, it seemed like my hearing had heightened to such

16

a degree that, although Rigel continued to speak, my mind was a vacuum barring any recognition of her voice. After a few minutes, she left. I couldn't help but sit there at the enclosure, wondering what to do.

The shock was overwhelming. I could feel the disappointment breaking through my heart. That moment gave perspective to how my life would proceed for the remainder of the year. I pushed it all away, got back on my feet, and walked back to Kevin and Mark with nothing to say. What was done was done, but Rigel's constant presence and memories revolved around my mind for the rest of the year. She became an infatuation, and I was reluctant to let go.

Our friendship soon came to an end—or rather felt as if it never had been. Normal conversations became awkward. Nearing the end of the year, the experience turned into a depression. My closest friends were aware of what was happening. I still remember the days I spent in isolation, drowning in my thoughts about her. I can't remember or justify exactly what caused me to like her. It was an infatuation after all, and I was overwhelmed by my feelings.

This first passion for a girl awakened my poetic ability. I'm an emotionally driven person. My mood, attitude, and thoughts reflect my emotions. I wrote a series of poems in dedication to—and inspired by—my crush on Rigel. It was from this experience that I adopted a nature to make people around me happy. I would crack jokes or tease people as I had done with Tina. By distracting myself, I was able to let go of my feelings for Rigel.

Kevin and Mark, concerned by my attitude to this issue, both advised me to forget Rigel. I listened to them and eventually accepted that it would have never worked out between the two of us. Matters were made worse when I learned that she had taken advantage of my friendship and my feelings for her. Through this experience, I learned that true love is an entirely different affair. When true love found me, it turned my life upside down.

The annual three-month summer vacation was around the corner. It was another blooming opportunity to put the past behind me. I knew that my experience with Rigel would always have a mark in my memory. I kept a picture of her in my wallet for the rest of the vacation. It became a reminder of what I had once felt for her—but also of the reality that I should never again become a victim of my own feelings in friendship or in love. It just wasn't me to keep myself down and depressed. I didn't want to fall into that void again. At that point, I was asking for too many things at the same time, but I soon understood that falling, in life, is sometimes the first step toward greater aspirations.

CHAPTER 3

MOVING ON

"It's a simple formula: take one step forward from the past,
and you will awaken new opportunities in the future."

When summer vacation arrived, my family and I visited my grandmother in our hometown, Madurai, India. It took a few days for the reality of time away from school, my friends, and Rigel to sink into my daily life back home. I felt as if I had registered at a rehabilitation center, a statement not to be taken negatively.

In Sudan, during the school year, I focused on my studies. This would leave me with the weekends and a few spare moments during the day to engage with my family. Everyone was busy with their own agendas. Dad would be immersed at work, Mom would be busy with housekeeping, Annie would be busy being herself, and I would be busy being a nerd.

Summer vacation had always been a great time for quality family bonding. I had lived in Tamil Nadu until I was ten. Tamil Nadu is a South Indian state, located across the Indian Ocean, above Sri Lanka. I was also part Sri-Lankan from Dad's side of the family, dating back a few generations. During the three years we had lived in Sudan, we returned to Madurai for our annual vacations.

We lived behind my grandparents' house. Our house was large compared to most traditional South Indian residences. We named the house after my grandmother Sampurna, Dad's mother. She had passed away in 1991, the year of my birth. The house was a tribute of sorts to Dad's hard work and played an important role in the history of my family and my parents' marriage. I'll keep that story for later.

A beautiful garden led to the entrance. The walkway was cemented and carved a path through the lush vegetation on both sides. Coconut, papaya, and mango trees—as well as the flowers and plants set up in the courtyard—provided a pristine, albeit, unintentional, image of a summer resort. Together with my grandparents' house, the two buildings took quite the space in our closely knit neighborhood. It also meant daily gardening activities for Annie and me.

I had countless memories of my childhood, playing in the garden while assisting Grandpa Antony and walking in his company to school. But due to my family's transfer to Egypt when I was only ten years old, my memories at home were limited. I also lost the opportunity to obtain a true sense of "home" in India, although I would like to return to Madurai to settle down in the future. Now, it just felt great to be back in my hometown again.

A few weeks into May, I was slowly making progress in accepting my experiences with Rigel the prior year and moving on. In the company of my family, I felt comfortable and at ease. I was back on track with my own life, and I liked the vibe of it. That was when I received a Facebook message from her. I had made an account upon the insistence of my friends at KAS since a few of them were not returning to school for the following year because their families had been transferred to other countries.

After seeing her profile picture, I recognized her as the president of the KICS MUN team, from the conference a few months ago. I was surprised that she actually remembered me after all these months. We never had the chance to talk with each other on a social level during the course of the debates. My first impression of Rina, during her speech at the initiation ceremony for MUN, was that she was very professional. She had an authoritative personality and a worthy leadership presence among her peers; it was obvious why she was the president of the school's MUN team. When it came down to business during the debates, she was an excellent competitor and a tough opponent.

I didn't hesitate to reply to her friend request. That was the start of a new friendship. I liked the opportunity to make a new friend. Our friendship grew uniquely through online contact, and we communicated through frequent e-mails and chat room discussions. During the summer, Rina told me she would be visiting India. She was Tamilian and would be meeting her family friends at Chennai, the capital of Tamil Nadu.

Through further arrangements, we decided that her visit would offer a chance for us to meet since my family was intending to travel to Chennai during the week of her arrival. It felt as if everything was going according to plan, and I couldn't help but feel excited. But, as usual in life, something had to come up.

Dad's plans changed drastically once we reached Chennai. In reality, we spent only three days in the city and had to return to Madurai as soon as possible due to some urgent pending work. It was hectic as we tried to accomplish what had originally been planned for a week in the span of three days. I received at least three calls from Rina during those three days about meeting up. I felt guilty that I had to say no on all three occasions. Once we returned to Madurai, I couldn't hide my disappointment about not having met up with her. We would have to wait until we returned to Sudan.

Having something to do while I was home kept my thoughts about Rigel at bay. I was getting closer to letting go and moving on from my memories of her. The expansive space at home proved advantageous to this. It provided me the isolation and solace I required. Mom and Dad often left home on family business, including visits to the bank or the land assets we had bought in nearby cities. Grandma Mary (Mom's mother) and Annie usually spent their time together in the kitchen or watched TV in the main hall.

As the sun scattered its fading light along the horizon and the cool drafts of the evening air hit the windows, I stole away to spend time on our terrace. Such moments often inspired me to turn a lot of my thoughts into poems and get in touch with myself. These lonely sessions also helped me understand the fallibility of my infatuation for Rigel. I realized that we were never meant to be; I found myself seeking a reason why I had ever liked her in the first place. The greater the realizations, the more they helped me move along. By the time we were to return to Sudan, I had comfortably moved on from my yesteryear experiences.

I found it difficult to accept that this would be my last year of school. I had finally made it to twelfth grade. Time had passed by so fast. It seemed like yesterday when I had enrolled at KAS and met my friends. On August 12, 2008, we flew back to Sudan. I was eager to begin my final year at KAS. *Comme d'habitude,* we decided to depart only a few days before school reopened. Classes would begin on August 15. Mom and Dad thought three days would be ample time to settle down and unpack. Surprisingly, as fate would dictate (note the sarcasm), it took us an entire week instead.

I was content to be back in Khartoum. The familiar sandy texture of the air, the low-cut horizon, and the warm winds of Sudan welcomed us eagerly. Clearing customs and making it to our car was a pain in the butt. In Sudan, there are several formalities for domestic passengers in general. We knew we were in for a long ride at customs since we had purchased an enormous amount of Indian goods and other miscellaneous items from extensive shopping sprees during the summer. This was enough of a reason for our baggage to be inspected by the customs officials, prolonging our exit from the airport.

By the time we were out of the terminal, Annie, and I were living role models of the walking dead. Due to exhaustion and fatigue from the long journey, we were literally falling asleep on our feet. I knew it was probably worse for Mom and Dad; they had to deal with all the formalities at customs. The ride home was a vague memory.

The familiar sight of our street and apartment building provided enough motivation for Annie and me to use the last reserves of our strength to carry the luggage up the stairs to our apartment on the third floor. We had an amazing apartment, a wonderful landlord, a beautiful garden, and a swimming pool—everything except an elevator! Once we were in, Annie, and I couldn't care less about where we slept as long as we could fall asleep. Unpacking and settling down could wait.

We all woke up late the following day and soon got down to business. While Mom and I unpacked, Dad and Annie cleared up the house and did some general cleaning. Compared to Madurai, I felt more at home in Sudan. I contributed this feeling to my experiences as a growing teenager, while living in Sudan. I loved the view from our apartment. Across the street, a line of restaurants served food on a 24/7 basis.

Havana restaurant was one of the first few that were up and running when we had arrived in Sudan three years earlier. Now, things had dramatically changed. Somehow Khartoum had modernized tremendously during this short time. Our balcony would be a frequent venue for airplane sightings due to our building's five-minute proximity to the airport. I also greatly enjoyed my time whenever Dad, Annie, and I took a swim at the pool below, by the garden.

Mom and Dad had always felt that Sudan would be a new, better experience compared to the struggles we had faced in Egypt. Dad, in particular, encountered a lot of issues at work. He had hoped for a better work environment in Sudan, but that didn't exactly go as planned. It took a few years, but he eventually found some resourceful and trustworthy comrades at work, which certainly lessened his burdens.

On the other hand, Mom had been a housewife ever since her marriage. She was the family accountant, maintaining everything that was related to family business. She never really enjoyed her stay in Sudan since there were not a lot of outlets for her to explore. Cairo was essentially a metropolitan city, and Mom often had the freedom and chance to shop or hang out in her social circle. Sudan, as a developing country, still had a long way to go in that sector. Her life was limited to the apartment, justifying her yearning for company.

Annie was still young. She was six years younger than me, and I had just made it to the seventeenth mark that summer. She was adaptable to the changing environments and enjoyed living in Khartoum. She had been a baby when we were living in Cairo. Lucky for her, she just had to go through kindergarten and first grade. Meanwhile, I experienced a lot of racism and social segregation at CAC. I spent elementary and middle school in the company of the few friends who accepted me. It was an isolating environment. I hated it at first and wanted to return to India, but with Dad's support, I persevered and grew up to be a strong, independent individual.

Now, just a day back home and we were hit by a haboob: an enormous desert storm with towering waves of dark red sand. We all stood awestruck that evening on our balcony; the tower of sand hung right above the skyline. It looked like a sand tsunami.

But none of this seemed to matter to me when only a few days were left until school was to begin. I was anxious to see my friends.

CHAPTER 4

REUNION

*"Don't try too hard to walk on a straight line
because life will always throw a curveball."*

While Mom and Dad were occupied with settling down, Annie and I eagerly awaited our reunion with friends at school. I often found it difficult to get to sleep the night before school began. It wasn't any different this time as I lay in bed drowning in memories of my friends. At one point, I realized that August 14 would be my last not sleeping at night before the first day of school.

The small student population at KAS made one practically recognizable and well-known by everyone in the community. My batch, for example, had only twenty students who would comprise all of twelfth grade. As leader of the Student Community Services Group, I was admired by all the teachers. Through my hard work and academic success, I had also gained the recognition, respect, and support of my peers.

My academic success could be contributed to the friendly and welcoming environment at KAS since I had enrolled in ninth grade. Although we did have a few new student arrivals and some abrupt departures over the three years, my batch had remained a tight-knit family of friends. Unfortunately, our family would have to part ways in the near future.

Recalling the last three years of my life at KAS made me melancholic. Cindy, Lynn, Mark, Kevin, Hank, YJ, and everyone else—we were a handful. I could understand now why our teachers had a tough time dealing with us. I still had a hard time believing we had made it to our senior year. I'm sure our teachers were thinking, *Oh yes! We've made it to the last year, only eight more months of dealing with these hooligans!* Three years, but as I lay in bed that night, it felt more like three days.

I soon encountered the memory of my temporary farewell at the end of the previous school year. I had been good friends with YJ since ninth grade; though we rarely socialized, we mutually cared for each other. She was also a close friend of Rigel. YJ had spent the final weeks of eleventh grade, along with Mark and Kevin, trying to persuade me to forget Rigel. Thinking back to all of it, I felt like an idiot, but I suppose it happened to everyone. They were difficult times, yet my success in following my friends' advice only made me look forward to better things this year.

I like to think things over a lot. Most guys prefer to be spontaneous. I have to place myself in the lonely and unpopular category of being a lot more sensitive to my thoughts and feelings. I liked interacting with my own life. I enjoyed thinking about my actions and decisions; I often pondered my role in many situations. It was a medium through which I could relieve my emotions, critique my decisions, and accept my actions. It was also my biggest flaw— that sort of reasoning could easily overwhelm me—as it had in Rigel's case. It is also one reason why Annie refers to me as the *girl* in the family.

Annie is a self-proclaimed tomboy, and she lives up to that reputation. Even though she is only eleven years old, she is spontaneous and driven. Mom thinks I inherited Dad's dreamy personality, and Annie inherited her practical attitudes. Annie described it simply as, "You think too much—that's all."

After my long walk down memory lane, I was about to fall asleep when I realized I still had to revisit one last memento I had kept with me throughout the summer. Reaching over to my wallet on the bedside table, I found Rigel's picture. I could have easily thrown it out, but I chose not to.

The picture had lost its freshness, and her image was gradually fading away—very much like my memories of her from the previous year. I hoped I had truly found a way to seal my infatuation for her. In my heart, I could sense that everything was going to be fine and that this year had something new in store for me. I felt happy with such an insight, and I couldn't stop smiling as I fell asleep.

* * *

The first day of school was intense and gratifying. I could identify the familiar faces greeting me among the crowd gathered at the quad. At six foot one, I was easily able to spot my friends congregating by the outer rim of the assembly. The quad was the vantage point to all the other buildings in KAS. One would have to pass through the quad to gain access to the high school and middle school buildings by the cafeteria and volleyball courts. Within a few feet of the school entrance was the administration office, and the parallel construction of the kindergarten and elementary school buildings.

There was also a beautiful garden by the school entrance and administration building. It was a wonderful place to relax and was my preferred spot to pass the time during my hectic school life. I could easily recollect the countless times I had napped under the giant tree, rooted at the center of the garden.

Lynn was the first to notice my arrival. Her delight was obvious; she ran over and gave me a big hug. It was nice to see her again, and it felt perfect to begin the day with a warm hug from a close friend. Lynn and I were the same age, and even though I was a senior and she was a junior, Lynn was actually a month older than me. Lynn had one more year to graduate. We had been great friends ever since we met in tenth grade when she had enrolled at KAS. We had shared a special set of memories over the two years.

Lynn was undeniably one of the most beautiful girls at school. Her long black hair certainly hadn't receded and tousled my face as she hugged me. Taking my hand in hers, she walked me over to the seniors who were having their own reunion. They were all there: Mark, Kevin, Cindy, Hank, YJ, and Rigel. Giving a quick nod and receiving several handshakes and hugs from my friends and classmates, I finally turned toward Rigel. I had been waiting for this moment. Surprisingly, I was able to meet her eyes without any hesitation. I felt nothing in my heart; a smile and a hello were my only greeting. It seemed like the events of the prior year had never occurred. It made me feel better and stronger.

An opening speech was made by the superintendent. This was regular protocol. The speeches usually involved information about any new developments on the school's infrastructure, accommodations, and faculty. Each grade was assigned a specific homeroom teacher every year. Our homeroom teacher that year was the newly appointed principal, Mr. Wilson, who was also my science professor. Our initial task for the day was to assemble in his room where we would receive our course schedules and a summary of what the school year would hold, particularly for the soon-to-be graduates.

Mr. Wilson was a family friend as well as my mentor. I had great respect for him. He was intelligent and had guided my mathematics and physics studies for the last three years of high school. My goal was to obtain a PhD in astrophysics just like he had; my career would be in academia. But, among my peers, I socially identified myself as a philosopher seeking wisdom and meaning in my own life. Sounds clichéd, I know, but it's the truth.

Mr. Wilson's classroom also included the science laboratory. It was a common retreat where my friends and I used to spend our lunch breaks, given its proximity to the cafeteria. As we entered the classroom, we were astonished to see the entire lab had been refurnished. It was a damn good job, and the laboratory looked better than before. The superintendent had mentioned this during the assembly, but we hadn't expected that great of a change. Everything in the lab, with the exception of the tables and chairs, was refurbished or new.

It took awhile for everyone to settle down while we absorbed the room's details.

Mr. Wilson said, "So, how do you guys feel to be back together?"

Mark said, "Oh, man, Mr. Wilson! The lab looks great, and it is wonderful to see you again. But I'm tired of seeing the same boring faces in this batch for the past three years!"

His response made the class explode in laughter. Laughing along with my friends, I felt that life could never be better, but the day had just begun—and greater surprises awaited me.

After an hour, the seniors met with the juniors. I got my second surprise of the day when Tina entered the room. I was so excited that I literally wanted to run over and begin talking to her. I managed to stave off that emotion and gave her the queen's wave instead. There would be a lot of time in the upcoming year to catch up with each other. That day was probably the best of the entire year. It gave me ample opportunities to mingle with old friends and settle in with new friendships.

Later on, I learned about Tina's decision to continue her high school studies at KAS instead of KICS. We would become close friends, sticking together through everything we encountered during the year. It was a lucky bargain; by being Tina's friend, I made another. She would soon hold a special place in my heart. Her name fit her personality quite well: Rose.

Simply said, she was beautiful and cute. Her isolated personality was a trait that she guarded fiercely. The hidden, enigmatic character of her identity drew me toward her friendship. Over the days that followed, I realized the worth of our friendship; it helped me understand her personality and reconcile and confront my own. Together with Tina, our friendship gave way to beautiful memories that still make me laugh to this day. I didn't realize at the time how lucky I was to have met her.

The year also had its share of shocks. Only a week in, Rigel found herself a new guy. Although I personally didn't care and didn't want to—I never had an actual relationship with her—I couldn't resist feeling a twinge of jealousy toward the new couple. Their presence at every mundane lunch break made me moody. I was smiling to my friends, but I was seething inside.

I hadn't forgotten the depression and isolation I had experienced a few months ago. Now that I would be seeing her every day at school, I needed something to isolate my thoughts. The answer came without notice. My friendship with Tina and Rose started to grow. In their presence, I managed to find solace and even a distraction from other thoughts that troubled my mind. In contrast to the unusual, discomforting solitude I had endured the previous year, I found true happiness and comfort in the company of my friends.

Instead of dwelling on the sadness of my past, I began finding happiness by making others happy and residing in the comfort of their friendships. Coupled with my new outlook, I could sense the beginning of a new change in my life and personality. In the company of my family, friends, and all I loved, I gained salvation for my inner conscience. All of a sudden, life had more to it than I had perceived earlier. I came to the conclusion that life is what one makes of it. I realized every day, moment, feeling, and emotion were part of me.

My happiness, I cherished and remembered. My grief, I learned to overcome. My melancholy, I endured and speculated as means to challenge my thoughts and philosophy. My confusion, I embraced as a way of living life. I lived the questions I had; amid the uncertainty, I sought elegance. My ironies, I experienced; within the chaos, I sought truth and stability. Life became me.

These feelings reminded me of a wish I had made a few days after my birthday in the summer. Annie had laughed when I had revealed my wish; it had been for nothing but that *something good would happen* in the year to come. I was happy now because the wish was becoming a reality.

* * *

Mark, Kevin, and I had been friends since ninth grade. Over the years, our personalities had matured greatly. I was a loner in ninth grade. My experiences in Egypt had given me a certain aversion toward socializing with others. I preferred to suffer in silence.

Upon my arrival at KAS, I identified with the student community. Kevin was one of my first friends. His finger-breaking handshake was a reminder of our first meeting. I met Mark through Kevin. As the years passed, I helped them in various ways, especially in their academics. Their friendship also granted me the pleasantry of actually opening up and establishing social connections with others around me.

While we each had our opinions for our futures, our careers, and our lives, our friendship kept us together. Kevin intended to pursue medical studies, while Mark and I sought philosophical adventures. When I was a child, I had a knack for questioning events that occurred in my environment. That notion caught up in my later years, molding me into a philosopher. I spent most of my time isolated in my thoughts and imagination. I never had the chance to attend an actual philosophy or theory of knowledge class, but I spent my spare time scrutinizing articles and writing my own philosophical analyses on life, the world around me, and the people in it.

Mark and I often spent our weekends on the phone discussing and arguing our views on several philosophical concepts. We even had aliases; we named ourselves after Greek philosophers whenever we communicated our thoughts on certain impressions and ideas. I was Xenophanes, and he was Diagoras. We had no specific reasons for our choices, but we were satisfied that they sounded cool in a geeky way.

We would take some of our discussions and compare them from a scientific perspective with respect to the studies we aimed to pursue in the future: Kevin as a biologist, Mark as an evolutionary psychologist, and me as an astrophysicist. We enjoyed each other's company. Now, we couldn't help wonder how those days were approaching an end. The thought humbled the minds of several of my friends. Only a week had passed since school began, but we already felt the countdown of our last days together. Once the second week set in, the teachers began tormenting us with a huge sum of work. It was understandable that it was senior year, but it seemed that the teachers didn't want to go easy on us at all. What kindred spirits they were. I had separate courses from my classmates since I had completed the necessary preliminary studies for high school a year earlier. My final year was a mix of specialized studies and a few core courses, such as English and foreign language, that I could attend with my classmates.

Mrs. Wilson was my English teacher, and I was one of her favorite students. Mom had a master's degree in literature, and I couldn't deny feeling an attachment to the arts. My equal interests in philosophy and science were traits I inherited from Dad and Grandpa Antony. It certainly gave enough reason for arguments between Mr. and Mrs. Wilson on what career I should pursue in the future. Should I become an astrophysicist or an author and poet?

English class had its own set of memories. In Mrs. Wilson's class, I met another of my best friends—the same girl who would cry on my shoulder at our graduation—Cindy. Our first impression of each other was hilarious. Cindy joined the KAS community two years earlier when I was in tenth grade. She was of a Spanish heritage and a very quiet person. Those days, I constantly sat with Kevin or Mark in class. I noticed that Cindy rarely participated in any of the class discussions. There was speculation that her spoken English wasn't very good. This led me to the false assumption that her limited speech was restricted to her comprehension of English. I was proven wrong one eventful day.

Cindy and I remark joyfully about that occurrence whenever we are asked by others of our meeting and friendship. In fact, our strong friendship often provoked rumors about our relationship and quite some jealousy among others in the class. I was sitting next to Kevin that day. We were reading a philosophical article provided along with an in-class discussion exercise. Kevin and I felt at ease with the topic and were conversing heavily.

Cindy and Mark were sitting by the cushions near the edge of the classroom. We'd been placed in random pairs by Mrs. Wilson. Kevin and I were content to be chosen as a pair, but when we heard that Mark's partner was Cindy, we couldn't help but laugh at the difficulties Mark would have to face. The reality, on the other hand, was the exact opposite.

Cindy had some questions about the article that even Mark found difficult to answer. She took the alternative of approaching us, but not knowing me well, had faltered. Mark decided to call me in her place. Although I heard him say my name twice, I told Mark to wait and continued my discussion with Kevin.

Cindy then took the initiative and said, "Hey, handsome. Can you help me over here with this article?" I nearly fell off my seat when I heard Cindy say those words. Thank God she hadn't been too loud. I'm soft when it comes to girls. So what did I do? I put an abrupt stop to Kevin's discussion, turned my chair around, and started talking with her instead.

Mark and Kevin couldn't believe it; they were staring daggers at me throughout class. They found my abrupt turnover something like a betrayal. I could sense they were being sarcastic and continued laughing at the hostile atmosphere they were trying to instill against Cindy and me. Eventually, we grouped together and delved into further arguments about the article.

That was the beginning of my friendship with Cindy. It grew to a greater extent in eleventh grade; she was a source of great support throughout my struggles with Rigel. In eleventh grade, I also found out about her boyfriend. She didn't reveal that secret to me for a while.

The history behind their relationship and meeting is funny, but I don't wish to divulge the story. Though there was talk among others in our batch that my friendship would diminish due to her relationship with another guy, the results were the contrary. In fact, Carlos, and I became very good friends.

We met during the International Dinner, an event that KAS hosted annually. It was a wonderful opportunity to bring together the international families that represented the school's student body for an informal dinner. Tables and chairs were arranged in the small field across from the quad, as was a buffet with various foods and beverages from different communities.

While people spent their time eating dinner at the tables, the quad also posed as a stage with dancing, singing, and other theatrical performances. The event usually lasted until late at night; I found it a chance to meet up with people from other communities and make new friends.

That year in particular, I wasn't performing on stage and engaged in a game of basketball with my friends. I had been a player on the school's basketball team during ninth and tenth grade. I left the team in eleventh grade due to academic time constraints. Our school had won the interschool basketball competitions for two years in a row, and several of my buddies were on the team.

Eventually, I retired from the game to talk with Cindy, who was sitting in the bleachers. She had been conversing with another guy while I was playing. I had mistakenly assumed that he was one of her family relations. He became my substitute and took my position while I watched the game with Cindy. Since I was thirsty, she decided to get me a drink from the quad.

It would be quite a wait until she returned, since the quad was crowded. I resumed watching the game from the sidelines and had to commend the guy on his skills. Once in a while, I looked around to see if Cindy had returned. All of a sudden, I heard a resounding cry of pain. I turned around immediately to see the guy, who had been playing well so far, holding his fingers as if they were broken.

Giving up his position, he came over and sat next to me, nursing his arm. It wasn't a serious injury; the incident occurred fairly often in basketball. Someone had passed the ball to him, and his fingers had caught it at the wrong angle, causing them to bend back. I knew the pain, and I was sympathetic, but it was something he could live with. Having seen us together, he asked if I knew Cindy well. Curious to see where the conversation would lead, I introduced myself.

He said, "Has Cindy talked to you about me before?"

I said, "No."

I didn't know if he was trying to catch his breath or balance the pain in his arm, but after much digression, he blurted, "I'm Cindy's boyfriend, Carlos. Nice to meet you!"

Okay. That was a shock. I'd been focusing on the game while he talked, but those last few words got my attention. Now I was ready to listen to what he had to say; I am sure I had a very bemused look on my face. Carlos took that as a good incentive to begin his side of the story.

He knew a lot about me already via Cindy. I spent the entire time just listening to him relate his tale. After a few minutes, we ended our conversation and were about to go find Cindy when we saw her approaching from across the field. She had a huge smile on her face. It seems that she had been watching us throughout our conversation and had decided to stay put with the drinks until we were done talking with each other. By the end of the day, I had a new friend.

Carlos was twenty-three years old and already had a job. His family was acquainted with Cindy's family; I could see they were a sweet couple. At that point, winter break was about to begin. It would extend for at least three weeks. Cindy went to Spain for Christmas, and Carlos was alone in Sudan. He was disappointed about her departure and hung out with me instead.

Som Café was a pub located several blocks from our house. Mark and Kevin often used to hang out there during the weekends. Both of them had the habit of smoking, and the pub offered hookah, an instrument for smoking flavored tobacco also known as *Shisha*. I don't smoke and tended to dislike the place and its atmosphere.

During the winter break, Carlos and I met at the pub at least two times a week. Carlos also smoked but refrained from doing so in my presence. I didn't really mind it; I had gotten used to secondhand smoking while hanging out with Mark and Kevin.

Carlos and I usually shared information about our lives. He already knew about my history with Rigel, and it made for good conversation. There were also nights where it was mainly about trying to cheer him up during Cindy's absence. He was infuriated that I received responses and e-mails from Cindy, and he didn't. I believe Cindy was just trying to pull his leg, but I didn't know if the right course of action was to sympathize with him or just laugh it off. His attitude took a turn for the better once she returned. It wasn't that long of a break.

Now, in my final year, I was more eager to catch up with the couple and make one last set of memories before we parted ways. But we met an early obstacle to our goals. Just a few weeks into the term, Cindy and I agreed to be partners in a history project. The project focused on journalism and addressed the economic inflation and recessions in Zimbabwe. Given our close friendship, our collaboration on the project began sparking rumors. Being ignorant and carefree, I was unaware of the rumors until I heard about them from Cindy. In fact, even after learning the truth, I didn't care about the rumor at all. It was its source and the people behind it that made me furious. It completely changed my view of some of my classmates and one person in particular.

CHAPTER 5

OLD RUMORS,
NEW DEVELOPMENTS

"I always try to see the best in everyone; sometimes that's my downfall."

Ms. Ramone's classroom was located at the far end of the last row of buildings composing the high school department, which included the English literature, mathematics, and biology classrooms.

The class would be a cause to run for whenever I arrived late to school in the morning. The room was small, but spacious enough to accommodate an average student population of twenty-five. The school's ventilation systems were predominantly based on giant water coolers—with the exception of the newly refurbished laboratory, the administration building, and a few classrooms. Ms. Ramone's classroom had the reputation of the worst ventilation, unless you knew where to sit.

She had been teaching world history and social studies at KAS for several years. Her children also studied at KAS, and their family had lived in Sudan for quite a long time. Ms. Ramone and I had a wonderful teacher-student relationship, and I'd always enjoyed her classes, starting from Ancient and Modern History in ninth and tenth grade, African History in eleventh grade, and now Comparative Government in twelfth grade. Sadly, her stern attitude often overshadowed her entertaining classes.

My studious behavior was a trait she admired. During the parent-teacher conference in ninth grade, she playfully described me as a studying machine. She was also the supervisor of the MUN team the prior year and had vouched for my position as president. The classroom was arranged in five rows of tables and chairs for the students. I had the tendency to change seats every so often during class. I found an incentive to sit beside Cindy due to our collaboration in the group project and the necessity to complete in-class project assignments.

During one of these sessions, Cindy told me about the rumors. We had Ms. Ramone's class for our block period that day; it would last for an hour and a half instead of the standard fifty minutes. I was to present the current events of the week. It was a regular routine, in the beginning of class, for students to present and express personal ideas and opinions about world events recently featured on the news. After finishing my presentation, we continued working on our projects.

Cindy and I had separated the work evenly between each other. I took the journal articles, sat on one of the couches in the corner, and worked my way through the hour. It wasn't too long before she motioned for me to sit next to her. Rigel and her friends sat in the row behind us. Their eyes followed me as I walked over and sat beside Cindy. It felt like something funny was going on—some kind of inside joke that I didn't know about, and as time passed, I could sense that the group behind us was discussing something that had no relation to their project.

Their dulcet conversation began to distract me, and I started to lose focus when Cindy said, "They are talking about us. It's just a stupid rumor. They think we're going out behind Carlos's back or something."

I stopped working once I heard those words. Although Cindy remained unperturbed, I was taken aback and could feel my temper flaring. I hated it when people talked behind my back. Frustrated, I said, "Why would they even think that? Who started this?"

Cindy arched her eyebrows, silently advising me to lower my voice. "Well, the rumor has been around for some time. They know you're a good friend of Carlos. But now, at school, they see us sitting together, sharing lunch, and the walk we had around the track that evening together. And now, working on this project, I believe they just assembled the pieces and came up with this rumor!"

"That's bullshit. Who is behind this? Do you know, Cindy?"

"I think it wise that I don't answer that question at all," replied Cindy.

"Oh, come on, Cindy. You know I hate it when people talk behind my back. To make things clear, I hope you aren't hurt or uncomfortable about any of this. Please don't take the rumor seriously because I have no such intentions."

"You think I would seriously believe this shit. You're one of my best friends. I know you better than anyone—and you know me better than anyone too. It would be stupid of me to doubt you. I trust you, and so does Carlos. Don't worry and forget about the stupid rumor."

I was relieved to hear Cindy say this, but I wasn't satisfied with her answer. She was still evading my question. "Thanks, Cindy. It means a lot to me that you and Carlos trust me to such an extent. I'm grateful to have you as my friend, but you're still as good as ever at evading an argument. Who started this rumor? Just tell me. I can take it. Is it someone I know?"

I could see the disappointment on her face and sensed the reluctance in her response. "Well, actually … um … it … er … it was Rigel."

That revelation stunned me. I remained quiet for the rest of the class. Cindy refrained from mentioning anything after that. The shock on my face was enough of a sign for her to remain silent about the issue. My mind was reeling. I couldn't believe that Rigel had done such a thing. My passive nature toward others, my willingness to see the best in everyone, had gotten the better of me again. I was distraught by the end of class.

In desperation, Cindy said, "I'm sorry. I know you liked her—a lot. After all that happened last year, damn it. I shouldn't have told you at all."

Cindy's words did not register in my ears. Once again, I was lost in my own world. I spent the lunch break alone at the garden by the administration building. Lying on the cool grass under the shade of the tree, I closed my eyes and drowned in my thoughts. I didn't understand why it always had to turn out this way. Why did people have to equate my friendship with Cindy to such scenarios? Couldn't a guy just be a genuine friend to a girl? And most of all, what was it in my personality that made me so vulnerable to being used and hurt by others?

I hated these thoughts. They hurt and planted doubts in my mind. If my presence and friendship was truly causing tension for Cindy and Carlos, what was I to do? She had brushed away the rumor earlier, but she could have done so in respect for our friendship. How could I be sure she was telling the truth? I remembered Mark and Kevin's criticism of my blindness toward Rigel using my feelings for her own benefit. It was all clear to me now—all of it. It was like seeing the girl I had once been crazy for in a different light.

I met Carlos that weekend when the Student Community Services hosted a party at school. As an active team leader, I had several responsibilities. These included making arrangements for food and drinks and monitoring the event. The quad was sanctioned off as a dance hall that night, and the DJ was doing a great job. The drinks were kept at the lab.

I enlisted the help of a few guys, including Hank and Carlos, to carry the cases back to the quad. I had talked with Carlos earlier that evening about the rumors, but his advice was to ignore the remarks. His take on it was that people were being stupid and jealous about my friendship with Cindy. Knowing that he had come to visit Cindy at the party, I decided to relieve him of assistance and recruited Dan to take his place.

Dan was a good friend, but at times annoyed the heck out of me. Hank and Dan were close friends and shared a brotherly bond.

Dan also knew everything about my history with Rigel. News spread pretty fast in a small community like KAS. While Hank and I took our time arranging the cases, Dan began taunting me about the rumors. At first, it was just light humor, but the comments abruptly took a wild turn.

We were on our way back to lock the lab after setting up the last cases at the dance hall. We stopped midway across the field when Dan's taunting reached a critical point. I couldn't ignore his remarks. I could feel my temper rise again and had a strong sensation of wanting to pummel Dan. Hank wanted no part in the conversation, but he felt the tension. He immediately put a stop to the discussion and told Dan to remain silent.

Pulling me away, he walked me back to the party. By that time, I was seething and my fists were clenched. It took me awhile to get a hold of myself.

Apologizing for Dan's remarks, Hank said, "I know Dan can be an idiot at times. But he didn't mean it. You were quite tense back there. I was afraid you were actually going to jump him at one point. If I were in your shoes, I would have had a tough time holding back too. I apologize once again on his behalf. Look, enjoy the party, relax for a while. You've done enough work for today."

I took a deep breath and turned around to face Hank. He didn't have to apologize or explain his friend's actions. Hank meant well. I didn't want to ruin his night on account of my own problems. Smiling, I said, "Thanks, buddy. But you know I shouldn't be ruining this for you either. It's a great night, and we both deserve a treat. Let's go!" I gave Hank a quick pat on the shoulder, and we returned to the dance. The night went well, but this rumor was really getting on my nerves. I prayed to the Almighty that it wouldn't get any worse. I just needed a break.

The following day, I was welcomed by an opportunity to meet Rina. Nearly a month had passed since we had returned to Sudan. I hadn't forgotten our plans for setting up a social, but we found it difficult to have some time apart from studying once school began.

Rina's family lived in a distant sector of the city's interior. From what I had heard in our countless conversations during the summer, her father had restrictions on her social life. She could only meet her friends under special occasions. I was lucky that Mom and Dad were quite the opposite. Dad encouraged me to find a means of recreation aside from academics. I was open with my family about my social life at school—with the exception of my fiasco with Rigel in eleventh grade. I felt guilty hiding it from them. It would have been easier to simply let them in on the truth, but I'd wanted to handle my problems independently.

After a quick chat on the phone, Rina, and I decided to meet for ice cream at Tutti House at seven o'clock. Tutti House was five minutes away from my apartment. It was one of my favorite spots to hang out with my friends. I left home at six o'clock and reached the restaurant within ten minutes.

Reserving one of the tables at the front, I waited patiently for Rina's arrival. I had received a call from her informing me that her father would bring her along, but now he was delayed at work. I'm not the kind to spend a lot of money when I venture out. I visited Tutti House frequently, but it was rare that I ate any ice cream there. The restaurant had also been a resort when I was depressed or needed some fresh air. The downside was its proximity to the airport. This resulted in consistent noise pollution due to the frequent arrivals and departures of flights.

Rina arrived at the restaurant at 7:15. Due to my height, I was easily able to spot her walking toward me. Waving in acknowledgment, she joined me at our table and gave me a warm hug. We were soon caught up in conversation about our lives after returning to Sudan. I was surprised to hear that Rina knew about my story with Rigel. I was further astonished that she was willing to be so open about her social life and circle of friends. At one point in the evening, Rina's friends dropped by the restaurant to make an order. Rina panicked as they approached our table. I was assured by her actions that she would hate if any stupid rumors were brought up because of our outing. She confirmed my thoughts when she made a pact that our relationship was solely as friends.

Rina's father picked her up at ten. We made a deal to meet every week if possible. I'd enjoyed my time with her. It felt refreshing to meet someone outside my regular circle of friends. It provided a new perspective to my life. I felt secure that there wouldn't be any rumors about our meeting, but life proved me wrong again.

Dan, that idiot! I was in a fury and wanted to kill him the following week. His girlfriend was a friend of Rina, and he heard about our meeting over the weekend. It didn't take him long to open his mouth and spread the news that I was "seeing" someone new. Can't a guy just have some privacy?

The majority of my friends knew the truth about my meeting with Rina. Nevertheless, they couldn't resist the urge to tease me in having found a new "girlfriend." For Lynn, Rose, Cindy, and Tina, their sole objective was to annoy the living hell out of me on this subject. These rumors would mean trouble in the future, but thanks to my shortsightedness at that time, I was able to convince myself to remain ignorant and maintain my poker face. It was a grave mistake on my part, but that wasn't the end of the story. Life still had several surprises in store for me that month.

* * *

Hank and I had been friends since ninth grade. We had both enrolled as new students at KAS that year. Initially, there was little communication between us, partly due to Hank's difficulty with spoken English. We became close friends during my age of depression in eleventh grade.

I spent my last day of eleventh grade with Hank. There weren't any official classes going on, but Hank had an extra exam to complete. I had to return books at the library. We hung around at school till noon, alternating between resting, talking, and playing basketball. I told Hank everything about my fiasco with Rigel while addressing my struggles to get her memories out of my life. That day made a great difference in strengthening our friendship.

My discovery about Hank and Tina's relationship was a wonderful experience. I didn't know how or when it happened, but I had seen it coming. The three of us, along with Rose, spent our lunch breaks together. During such moments, I became suspicious of Hank and Tina's relationship. Often I found myself in Rose's company while the other two wandered off on "a walk around the school." Eventually, I couldn't hold back suspicions. Taking my chances one day, I sat with Tina and asked her to tell me the truth. I had been expecting it, but I was still shocked to actually hear that they were dating.

The turn of events under which they came together remained mysterious, but the fact that they were now a couple was happy news. Our discussion also revealed the obvious cons of their relationship. Tina's family was conservative and strictly traditional. They didn't approve of her relationship with Hank. Our conversation also sparked a few doubts in my mind, drawing parallels to a talk I had earlier with Carlos and Cindy.

I considered Tina to be like my younger sister. I knew our close relationship was vulnerable to the misguided eyes of other students. I was afraid that a relapse of events, similar to the rumors of my relationship with Cindy, could happen in my friendship with Tina. My doubts on this issue were quelled when they were addressed by someone I didn't expect to confront: Hank.

Hank's misunderstandings developed in the presence of my close friendship with Tina. I had heard about his reservations from Tina at the end of Spirit Week. Spirit Week was an annual tradition at the school and involved a week of interactive extracurricular activities focusing on physical education and sports. Classes and activities were shuffled throughout the day. The small student population at KAS made it easy for the teachers to host such an event and separate the students into teams.

Tina and Hank were placed on different teams, but Rose and I were together. The games seemed to go on forever. By noon, I was thoroughly exhausted. During the break, Tina persuaded me to join her on a visit to the school garden. The games would continue very soon, but Tina's persistence and tone compelled me to accompany her. We spent an hour together while Rose and Hank enjoyed the games.

In the garden, I lay down on the grass. Using my cap to shade my eyes from the glaring rays of the sun, I fought a strong urge to nap. Tina sat beside me on a broken tree stump, warning me not to fall asleep, lest I suffer her wrath. It didn't help as she stayed silent for a long time. I remained stoic, patiently observing the passing clouds. After what seemed an eternity, she began talking. She had some difficulty expressing her thoughts, but eventually admitted Hank's doubts and suspicions about the nature of our friendship. Having foreseen such a scenario, I felt it was ironic that my life seemed to revolve in a circle.

In ninth grade, I preferred isolation to friendships, partly so that I could spare myself from having to deal with these issues. I discarded such notions once I was accepted by everyone in the KAS community. With Tina, I was reconsidering that decision. Hank's misunderstandings varied widely and focused on my cordial and intimate friendship with Tina. I didn't want to hear any more about it. I proposed to Tina that it was my fault and suggested maintaining some distance in our friendship.

Tina, in denial, implored, "I will talk to Hank about this. There is no need for us to maintain a distance in our friendship just because of Hank's doubts. You're like my brother! I was reluctant to discuss this with you, but I would be concerned if you two have a confrontation. I don't want your friendship with Hank to go down the drain because of his misunderstandings or because I'm his girlfriend. I will talk to Hank and make sure he gets this, all right? Cheer up. Let's head back to the games."

Tina's response was humbling. I was happy that I'd found an understanding friend, but I knew it would only make things worse if she addressed this issue. I decided it would be best for me to sort it out with Hank. I refrained from sharing my intentions with Tina, and we returned to the games. The rest of the evening passed in bliss, but I couldn't help wonder how many more situations I would face with my friends in the near future and under similar circumstances. It was important that I resolved this issue as soon as possible.

Our confrontation took place one evening after school. Hank and I had been stood up by our drivers. The school was empty, save for the two of us in the parking lot. Shaded from the searing heat of the evening sun, we were isolated in our own thoughts.

But then, Hank said, "Are you and Tina like really close or something?"

I was relieved that Hank posed the question. In response, I said, "Tina told me everything, Hank. I can't deny that I was a little hurt when I heard about your misunderstandings. We are good friends. How could you think like this? I don't mean to hurt you, but you know that Tina and I are like brother and sister. We met at KICS during the MUN council last year. We are close friends—that's all. I have no other intentions for Tina. There's nothing going on between us."

Silence accompanied these words. I was glad to see signs of regret on Hank's face. It meant that we had resolved the issue after all. After a while, Hank apologized.

"I'm an idiot. I'm sorry, bro."

That was good enough for me. Laughing, I slapped Hank on the shoulder and said, "It's all right, buddy. I understand."

His apology didn't mean that he was at fault. It was a stupid misunderstanding that could happen to anyone. I was content that he had the courage to resolve the issue directly with me. Altogether, the experience formed a greater bond of brotherly camaraderie between us. Along with Rose and Tina, we stuck together as a fixed group of friends. Having overcome our doubts and our misunderstandings, our friendship and mutual love grew even stronger.

I spent every day at school in their presence. Their friendship was a spiritual form of support. We frequently stayed two or three hours after school whenever we could spare the time. The girls would usually be the first to leave. Tina's driver was an idiot who often arrived early before school ended at two o'clock. Hank, Rose, and I consciously delayed Tina from leaving so she could spend more time with us. For all of us, time was valuable. Hank, and I, in particular, were to graduate at the end of the year, and we wanted to optimize our time with Tina and Rose.

The cafeteria was one of our common hangouts. Hank and Tina would flirt on one side, and Rose, and I would indulge in laughter and our own conversations. Our moments together would spell new beginnings.

I wanted to know more about Rose—not just as a friend, but as the person she was. Like her name, she was as beautiful a girl as I had ever seen, but also shy and enigmatic. I wanted to understand and learn more about her personality and life. In my heart, I felt that we were similar. This attribute drew me to her. Only the necessity of our own realizations stood in the way.

The cafeteria was situated on a plane of colored stones and pebbles spread widely under the shade of a large tree. I adopted a funny nature with Rose and loved to tease her. She literally brought out the jokester in me, and I wouldn't give up on any opportunity to lovingly annoy her. On several occasions, Rose and I found ourselves on opposite sides, supporting the dominant couple in our group. Tina and I, as "brother and sister," would frequently unite against Rose and Hank whenever we had arguments. We maintained the upper hand at all times, often silencing the other duo into verbal submission. At the end of the day, it was just a lot of fun and laughter.

Being with them made the difference. Whenever we needed some isolation, we would spend time together at the garden. Tina and Hank would wander off, leaving me with Rose. We would converse, while I would nap on the grass. Bit by bit, I realized that through our secular moments together, Rose and I were getting closer in our relationship. I wondered if she realized it too.

Everything seemed to work out perfectly. Life, at that moment, was just getting better and better. Remember, I'm one to let emotions dictate my life. Well, this new happiness inspired me to write poetry again. In fact, it all started with Rose's request.

I enjoyed my time with Rose, but my teasing nature sometimes landed me in trouble. Jokesters better know their limits. Rose taught me that firsthand. She had been a talented receiver of my jokes. She knew I meant no harm when I teased her. One day, it got out of hand and—to make things worse—Tina and Hank had run off on a romantic escapade. We were at the library that evening. I don't know what I said or did, but I knew something was wrong when I didn't hear her usual laughter.

Normally, I can handle such situations and ease the tension gradually, but Rose was the type to express anger via silence. I fumbled in such scenarios. She might as well have killed me there. The atmosphere felt similar to defusing a bomb. To add insult to injury, I couldn't recollect what I had exactly said. I maintained an awkward silence, trying to figure out what I had done wrong. Rose sat beside me, staunchly looking in the opposite direction.

Phoebe from *Friends* often said, "Men are really good at saying mean things to women and not even caring." Her words perfectly described my situation.

A few minutes later, Rose moved to another table; this elevated my fear of wanting to apologize. It would now involve the desperate journey of walking over to her.

The library was to close in a few minutes. It was time for us to leave, but I couldn't imagine the day proceeding on this note.

Before she left the table, I rushed over and held her hand and stuttered an apology.

"Hey, I'm sorry. I know I went off limits. I'm sorry, Rose."

She looked over me sternly for a few minutes. The silence was truly killing me by then. But I was relieved when she broke into a smile and said, "Okay. Just don't do it again. I can't believe it took you that long to apologize."

At this point, my mind recited the words, *Well, if you weren't so scary.* But they certainly weren't suitable for this moment. Rose's playful slap on my shoulder brought me back to reality.

She said, "Anyways, forget what happened."

Once again, I could hear the voice in my head, as it said, *I have that covered; I can't even remember what I'd said in the first place.* I was strangely aware of the bemused expression on my face due to the ongoing conversations with Rose and in my head.

"Now, let's get a move on before they close up," she added, and I didn't hesitate to follow her.

A few days after this, she abruptly declared a new nickname for me: "Best friend." On these terms, she gradually began to open up about her personal life. I made a silent promise, in our friendship, to remain honest and truthful to her and my feelings. It had been a slow process, and I had almost given up, but this new turn of events kept me hopeful.

One day, she asked me to write a poem for her. It was during our lunch break. It was a normal day, and the sun was making its presence felt at noon. Thanks to the natural ventilation, a cool breeze swept through the cafeteria.

Rose was sitting across the table, watching me eat, occasionally making a remark about something and tending to her windswept hair. Any guy would have taken the opportunity to admire her beauty, but I was savoring my curry instead. I nearly choked, when I heard her request.

"A poem? Why all of a sudden?"

"You're a poet, aren't you? So write something about me—what you feel or what you think of the person you know as me. Take as long as you want to."

She said this with a flirtatious smile. With a rice-ball stuffed in my mouth, I knew I looked like a goof while I sat there blushing and suddenly feeling shy upon hearing her request. She soon left me behind and ran off to join Tina who had just returned from her walk with Hank. I couldn't help but smile on this new development. It seemed like it was the day I had been waiting for. I knew I couldn't miss out on this chance.

Returning home that evening, my focus was on writing the poem. I sat in my room for an hour, trying to figure out what to write. It was ridiculous that, after all this time together, I still couldn't find a hint, notion, or feeling to express my thoughts for Rose. I could hear the voice in my head saying, *Come on, dude. After all these days, you've got nothing on this girl? You are able to write three pages about a leaf falling from a tree in the middle of autumn, but not this? You're hopeless.*

That's when it hit me. I had nothing to work with. I still had no clue about her true personality, or who she was as a person. But I decided that was exactly what I needed to write about.

Thoughts within a Silence

Talking with you
Does make me feel
That I might not know everything about you.
Writing about you
Is a simple possibility,
But nevertheless a huge uncertainty, in the
words I might use to describe you.
But in the end,
You are complete,
Not in my words or through them, but in
my thoughts and in my heart.
Thinking of you,
Thinking of you,
All I can do sometimes is just think about you.
Talking with you every day,
Hearing your laughter,

A pleasure and happiness I will always remember.
I might not know a lot about you,
I might not know you at all,
But within my thoughts, you reside, complete above all.
One day became another;
One night became another.
That's how long I had to think to write about you.
Defined within my thoughts,
Defined in my mind,
Your identity, I realized, was something hard to find.
But eventually there came a day,
The questions were at an end,
And that night, the answers began to tumble.
60 minutes,
3,600 seconds,
I remained stationary in my thoughts, waiting for the feeling.
Those 60 minutes and 3,600 seconds,
You remained the unfinished painting,
And I, the desperate artist.
An ultimate silence,
An ultimate rendering
Gave way to a final feeling.
A final feeling,
And the initial word,
The writing began and the painting drawn.
Line by line,
Word by word,
I finally finished what I had.
This poem
Might not be about you,
But the experience and difficulty I had in writing about you.
Not because I don't know you,
Not because I can't describe you,
But because these are the thoughts of a silence.

A silence that I was enveloped in
When I thought about you,
And a silence that I hope I will get answers to, in the near future,
When I come to know you.

I gave the poem to Rose the following day. I expected a reply, but I didn't mention this to her. She was delighted about the poem and hurriedly stashed it away into her bag when Tina questioned her about it, promising instead to read it when she returned home.

A few days later after school, I was sorting through my backpack in my room when I found a letter safely hidden in one of the pockets. I was delighted to open it and find a letter from Rose, along with a poem.

Behind My Mask

Every morning I open my eyes,
Wondering if I would live through the day.
A journey of a thousand miles,
I start with a single step.
I look out to the world,
And realize that I stand alone,
Everybody is blind to what I see,
And deaf to what I hear.
They ask me,
Why am I who I am?
I answer only with stillness,
No friend to help me.
Betrayed once,
Twice,
Three times,
I'm breaking apart.
Someone enters into my life,
But not into my heart.

Betrayal of trust and acceptance of who I am,
I hide in fear behind my mask.
I built walls around me,
High and strong,
Who knows what's inside?
My heart is open to no one.
I smile,
I laugh,
Hoping to hide the tears,
Behind my mask.
I run and run,
To numb my pain,
I welcome the loud beat of my pulse,
And silence the sound of my heart shattering.
I stand strong,
My head kept high,
But how long could it last?
My weak heart and breakable mask.
Every night I close my eyes,
Hoping to forget everything,
Praying for a savior,
To heal my broken heart.
I cry silently,
No one can hear.
Tears falling endlessly,
Behind my mask.
I'm about to give up,
I'm about to break down,
But a voice asks,
Why did I hold on for so long in the first place?
My dreams have shattered into thousands of pieces,
I pick one of those pieces and start over.
My failure has made me pathetic,
But remember that it's a stepping stone to something better.

Hey, best friend,

"Thoughts within a Silence" is gorgeously written. I couldn't help but smile as I went through each line. It's so honest and touching; I don't know how to describe what I felt when I read it. I love it and thank you.

I love poetry, but I suck at it. My poem is "Behind My Mask" and the story is right there in the title. I only took two hours to write this poem so it's bad. After I read your poem, I felt the urge to write one myself; it's not as good as yours. I sat blankly for fifteen minutes thinking of what to write about, and it took a lot of effort to make the decision to focus on "my mask."

I stared at my paper and chewed on my pen, frustrated. It took all my courage to open up my heart just a crack and start writing. I know it's a depressing poem, and I am, in truth, embarrassed. I don't know what made me open up my heart; I guess because you were honest and it moved me …

And that was when I realized I had struck a beautiful chord in my relationship with Rose.

CHAPTER 6

SWEET MELODIES

*"There's music all around us: in the capriccio of a young
maiden's love, in the harmonies of past memories, or
in your case, the dolce melodies of school life."*

When I read Rose's letter and poem, it felt like I was conversing with
an entirely different person. Her words clearly were from the heart,
and I was grateful that she was willing to share that part of herself—
no matter how small it was—with me. Somehow, her words made
me feel like I was important to her and that she could confide her
personal feelings in me. That definitely meant something for us.

As she had mentioned, I'd glimpsed a hidden part of her
personality. I had made a tiny crack in her heart, but it was one
from which I hoped to understand her better. I sealed the letter
and poem in a folder and secured it in a safe place. I intended to
keep them with me for a long time. A premonitory feeling made me
believe that one day I would cherish the words she had written to
me. All that mattered now was for me to take the step forward to a
new place in our friendship.

My objective met some difficulties. Apart from my social life,
I had a lot to deal with at school. Up till then, I had enjoyed the
company of my friends, but it was time to get down to business. It
was mid-November, and only a few days were left until our semester
exams. I had my share of responsibilities as an active member of
Student Community Services. I was also enrolled in Advanced
Placement courses for physics and calculus. That meant a lot of

homework. Coupled with the credentials I had to sustain in my other core classes and the supplementary work required for applying to university, it was a miracle that I had been able to slack off for so long.

Thanks to Grandpa Antony's genes, I had great organizational abilities. This gave me an advantage to the point where I could have a perfect balance between my academics and my social life. I had slacked off for a month, and it would be a little more difficult to get back on track this time. It didn't help to be an autodidact either. An autodidact is a self-learner. As such, I also enrolled in several independent studies at school. This meant that I would have to deal with a marathon of exams when the semester ended.

But it wasn't stressful. I enjoyed my studies, and that made a big difference. I had elective studies in Discrete Mathematics and Instrumental Music. Between the two, the latter was my favorite class. It was one of the few places where I could just be myself. My teacher, Ms. Lana, was someone I admired and considered a close friend. She was also somewhat of a parent-figure in my life at school, watching out for me like she did for her own son. This led to the growth of a wonderful bond between us. I was also close friends with her son John, who had left KAS two years earlier. It had been a difficult farewell.

I had been in Ms. Lana's music class for the first three years of high school. It was through Mr. Wilson's assistance that I was able to pursue further musical studies in tenth grade. The smaller student population made it difficult to enlist in specialized courses. It was a requirement to have at least fifteen students in a class. Thankfully, we were successful and a total of twenty students expressed interest in Ms. Lana's class. The class became popular in its introductory year (and continues to grow.) My experiences in Ms. Lana's classes have played a predominant role in motivating my interests and love for music.

She helped me discover my passion for music, and her classes gave me beautiful memories that I cherish. Grandpa Manuel (Dad's father) had been a musician, and as heredity would explain, Dad was also a musician and singer. Music was ingrained in my family. I had played the flute since middle school and had a keen interest in the piano. Music has had a great influence in my life. I have used the notes and melodies, while either singing or playing an instrument, as a medium to express my feelings and emotions.

Yep, I sing too! At that point in my life, I hadn't mentioned to anyone that I could sing. It was one of the few things I was shy about, but I couldn't hide it forever. Music caught up with me one fateful day.

Ms. Lana was organizing a musical based on Cinderella's story. *The Glass Slipper* required a scene where the prince had to dance with Cinderella. Dan was the prince! The song for the dance was "I'll Be Right Here Waiting for You" by one of my all-time favorites, Bryan Adams. John was partnered with Nina, another close friend of mine, for the accompaniment.

During the rehearsals, the duo had great difficulty in maintaining the higher modulations of the song. While John and Nina were "resting" their voices after a harsh set of rehearsals, Ms. Lana called me over. Setting the song on playback, she mentioned how she would have to prepare an alternative piece for the accompaniment, "There isn't anyone else who could take their place, and it is redundant to waste our efforts on a song that just doesn't seem to work out for John and Nina. They've both tried their best. I must find a new, suitable song with the limited time that is left. This will be difficult, as John and Nina would have to double their efforts in perfecting the new piece. I should have thought about this earlier!"

There were only a few days until the performance. It would be stressful for John and Nina to perfect the new song by then. I could see that there was a lot at stake. I had sung Bryan Adams before and knew this particular song very well. With no pretense, I immediately began singing along with the music. The reaction was felt five minutes later when I concluded my performance. John and

Nina, who had been napping by the couches, were looking at me as if they had never seen me before.

Ms. Lana sat by her desk, her mouth wide open.

Clearing my throat, I asked, "So was that good?"

"Good? Are you crazy? Why the hell didn't you tell us that you sing?" Nina yelled from across the room.

John said, "Bro, I'm going to kill you. Let me get this straight— the past few weeks, you've just been having fun watching us sing with parched throats, knowing all along you could have done a better job yourself?"

That was all to it. I was chosen as the lead singer, and the rehearsals continued. Ms. Lana was ecstatic. Letting me handle the higher modulations, John and Nina's spirits rested peacefully in the lower chords and harmonies of the song. For me, it was going to be my first official performance. The news spread pretty quickly.

On the night of the musical, my performance was a great success; everything worked out as planned. Ms. Lana was nearly in tears by the end of the night, which was a sign that she was very happy. John and I gave her huge hugs at the end of the show. We knew the troubles she had gone through to arrange everything in the musical, and we were happy for her success.

Nina and John left the KAS community at the end of tenth grade. Throughout the year, we continued singing together as a trio for musical performances. John and I composed several songs and melodies on the piano. We shared a common interest in music that extended beyond playing instruments. John's experience was built on his understanding of music; no matter what he played, it always felt like it came from the depths of his soul.

We also had our own share of funny moments. While playing the piano, John and I would sing whatever words came to our minds. It was our method for composing songs. We never really wrote down the lyrics or recorded the melodies, but we lived the music for the moment. Once, I remember being in Ms. Lana's room, rehearsing for the musical, playing the piano, and making good melodies. John suddenly decided to use one of the wireless microphones and posed as a performer. Unfortunately, the microphone was attached to one of the speakers outside by the quad. As John and I continued making lame jokes and lyrics, we were oblivious to the fact that the entire school was listening. It was embarrassing for us when we realized the truth, but it didn't stop us from joining in laughter with our classmates and Ms. Lana, who burst into the room once we had completed our "beautiful" composition.

These memories portray the close friendship, happiness, and passion we shared when it came to music. At the end of the year, as a token of our friendship, John, and I wrote a song to perform on the last day of school. The song depicted children and their symbolism as the hope for the future in a society beset by war, corruption, and poverty. John and I worked hard on the composition. The song was lauded by the teachers, parents, and fellow students. We were surprised to hear that a few parents had cried during the performance; a few even came by the music room to collect copies of the composition. John, and I never expected such a reception, but it was a memorable note to end with on our farewell.

The World's Out in Fear

The world's out in fear,
Little children feeling fear.
Blood everywhere,
It's not fair.
We should stand together,
Live forever,
Till the day,
Till the day,
We save this world from war,
Till the day,
Till the day,
We save this world from war.

One day I wrote a song
About the world all along.
To me it wasn't what
The world we know
It's all about,
Finding hope
So we live in peace.
The world's out in fear,
Little children feeling fear.
Blood everywhere,
It's not fair,
We should stand together,
Live forever,
Till the day,
Till the day,
We save this world from war,
Till the day,
Till the day,
We save this world from war.

Two years have gone by since these events, yet the melodies of our past—the fun, the laughs, and the refreshing memories—resound in my heart. Over this time, I learned the piano, exercised my abilities in the flute, and further strengthened my skills in singing.

In twelfth grade, Ms. Lana's class was modified into a choir. Singing experience was not required for the students who joined the class. Girls were the majority, but I was surprised that Cindy and Rigel had enrolled in the class. After John's departure, I was unable to find a friend who shared my passion for music. I believe it was a lucky coincidence when I met Rino during our first choir session.

Rino and I became immediate friends, partly due to his Indian background, his piano expertise, and his enthusiasm toward music. Soon, we began collaborating on compositions. Ms. Lana supervised us, offering her opinion and advice whenever needed. It felt like a recap of my musical adventures with John. My intuition and Rino's technical prowess on the piano offered us several opportunities to perform in music class, and we became Ms. Lana's prized students.

Rigel's presence didn't perturb me. The past had finally become the past, and I could begin living in the present. Three people helped me find my way back: Tina, Hank, and Rose. Rose, in particular, was an enormous contribution to this by motivating me and allowing me to be a part of her happiness. It astounded me to no end that she remained unaware of how her presence had completely changed my life. Ever since her letter, I looked forward to meeting her every day. I yearned to discover what the future held for us.

I maintained a false mask in the company of several of my friends, laughing with them on occasions, just for the sake of it. But with the support and happiness that I fostered in my friendship with Rose, I found the strength to attain an optimistic personality. It's interesting how someone could have such an impact on your life without realizing it—or you expecting it.

These dramatic changes kept me in good spirits for any upcoming challenges in my social and academic lives. A critical obstacle for me was the semester exams and additional practice exams for my AP courses. It was quite a challenge. Hank and I were working our asses off to pass our courses. I felt lightheaded and tipsy whenever I thought about the extensive paperwork I had to review for my exams.

Rose took this opportunity to turn the tables and began teasing me. Hank and I frequently vented our frustrations about the exams to Tina and Rose.

"I can't believe it. We're nearing finals, and we're having more tests than reviews. Mr. Wilson is killing me with all these assignments. Hey, Rose! What about you? Any tests? I have three tests coming up on three consecutive days. I think I'm going to be sick," I said exasperatedly. I was living the life of a perfectly apathetic student in that moment.

"Oh! I'm so sorry to hear that, but I think you dug your own grave when you took those AP courses. As for me, I don't have any tests, so I'll be going home to relax. No homework either. I'll probably head out to meet some friends this evening. Want to join us? Oh, I forgot you have to study," replied Rose with a sarcastic smile.

"Oh yeah? Speak for yourself! I should have been smarter about bringing this up to you! Doesn't anyone care about me?" I replied.

Hank was receiving similar treatment from Tina. We were in this dump for good, and it wasn't going to end until after exams.

In the first week of November, I got my chance to retaliate against Rose. I found out that her birthday was on Halloween. I regretted having missed out on the occasion, but I decided to give her a late birthday wish. I could only get so far to saying "Happy" before bursting into laughter every time I looked at her face.

Flustered, Rose sought an explanation, and I said, "Your birthday suits you. Scary people equate to scary birth dates, don't they!"

Her reply to my joke was the usual hard smack on my shoulder.

Exams were scheduled for the first week of December. Things were starting to get busy. I still found ample occasions to have fun with Rose; we even had a water fight after school by the cafeteria. I was hanging out with Hank and Tina. For no apparent reason, Rose doused me with a load of water from a water bottle she bought with my money.

Tina and Hank's raucous laughter filled the air in response to Rose's actions. Being a man, I couldn't take that lying low. Giving a smile to Rose, I slowly walked over to the cafeteria, bought two extra bottles of water, and headed toward her.

Rose began backing away and said, "Don't you dare!"

I emptied one of the bottles over her head.

Hank and Tina couldn't resist laughing, but they abstained from any involvement in the water fight. After Rose and I settled our scores, which involved a lot of chasing her around the school, we found them waiting for their rides by the school parking lot. We were soaking wet, but the water fight actually helped counteract the heat wave that hit Khartoum that afternoon.

Once I returned home, I had no intention of studying, but I kept busy by texting Rose as we playfully continued our argument.

* * *

The stress eventually took a toll on me. AP Physics was my toughest class. I enjoyed the course, but the weekly tests and lab reports made it difficult. I was experiencing extreme mood swings; at one point, I regrettably lashed out at Lynn. I was discussing the solution to a particular problem with my classmates. From what I recall, Lynn had dropped in to seek help on the same problem. I had, in the heat of discussion, shunned her. I must have said something really stupid because it left her in tears at the end of the day.

I had never meant it; to make it worse, I didn't realize my mistake beforehand. I was astonished by her sulky attitude after class and decided to talk to her after school.

Catching her at the parking lot, I asked, "Lynn, what's the problem? You've been ignoring me since physics class. I came by to say hi during the break, but you just walked away. Are you angry with me or something? If you are, please tell me what I did wrong."

I couldn't believe myself when I heard the story. It certainly didn't sound like me to have shunned Lynn in that manner. I hated it when I let the stress get to my head or let my frustrations get the better of me. I always tried to maintain patience in any scenario, knowing I would only hurt those dear to me if I gave in to my anger. I was guilty as charged, and I didn't hesitate to apologize.

"I'm so sorry, Lynn. It's just ... I'm under a lot of stress. I'm graduating this year, and there are so many responsibilities. It doesn't help to have assignments and exams on top of that. You know I would never want to hurt you. I apologize on this occasion." My words were falling on deaf ears; Lynn's visage was stoic. "Hey, look here. I'm sorry for what I did. I would never hurt you on purpose.

I know I'm an idiot, and I know I may be asking for too much right now, but I'd like it better if you could smile and accept this poor man's apology. Plus, you look even more beautiful when you smile." I looked directly into Lynn's eyes and gestured as if praying for forgiveness.

Those last few comments cheered her up, and things were back to normal. The following day, we had our AP Physics test. In order to lighten up the atmosphere after an intense forty-five minutes of physics, I made possibly one of the best jokes of my life. Mr. Wilson and I often argued about politics, metaphysics, and other subjects that caught our interest. His general knowledge was so vast that, in most cases, I had a difficult time dealing with his counter remarks in our rhetorical encounters. But, after four years of his tutelage, I had finally—in a naïve sense—surpassed him.

Mr. Wilson had a knack for teasing the students in his class, especially me. As we filed out for lunch that day, he told everyone to stay put and turned in my direction. With a sarcastic smile, he said, "Boys and girls, I don't want to see any of my AP Physics students, especially him, interacting with AP Literature students. You should understand that we are in a different league compared to them."

Mr. Wilson's rivalry with his wife was an old issue. She was the instructor for AP English Literature and Composition. Mr. Wilson knew of my interests in the arts and enjoyed teasing Mrs. Wilson—or anyone else who studied the subject. His antics were usually received with sarcasm and ignorance.

But I wasn't ready to let him off the hook so easily. I said, "Now hold on, guys. I don't think that's fair. Mr. Wilson, we will agree to your deal, if and only if, you take on ours. We don't want to see our AP Physics instructor flirting with the AP Literature instructor during lunch either. If you're game for that, it's a done deal."

The laughter was deafening. Rino and several of my classmates were patting me on the back. "Hear, hear! Mr. Wilson, you got anything to say to that?"

Lynn was laughing, using my shoulder for support. Mr. Wilson was blushing to the extreme. Embarrassed as he was, he handled the situation very well. He said, "Touché, my young padawan." It was one of the rare occasions where I was able to beat Mr. Wilson in an argument.

Lunch was a fiesta; my classmates treated me like a king. Mr. Wilson continued "flirting" with Mrs. Wilson during the break, but when she heard about what had happened, she high-fived me and laughed with us.

Studies aside, November was passing slowly. I began ruing the day school would end for winter break. I was confident about my upcoming exams. Apart from the core classes, the AP practice exams were to take place a week earlier than originally scheduled. Despite the studious atmosphere, there were still pockets of entertainment. The International Dinner was planned for the last week of November. It was an event to look forward to before jumping into the quicksand called semester exams.

In English class, I was occupied in philosophy with Kevin and Mark while reading *Hamlet*, possibly my favorite Shakespearean play. French class ran on a similar note. Our French instructor was a kind woman. She wanted her students to enjoy the class while achieving something. Thursdays were pancake days and movie sessions; the class would watch a French movie while a few others would prepare pancakes. I had known my French instructor for four years; under her guidance, I had dramatically improved my fluency in French. I was going to miss her entertaining classes after graduation.

There was one early-release day during November. School ended at eleven o'clock. While waiting for my ride, Lynn pulled me into an isolated room so we could talk about something personal. Cindy, Kevin, Mark, and a bunch of other classmates began teasing us about what we had been doing inside the room for so long. All jokes aside, nothing had really happened. Sometimes I felt that my friends seriously needed to get a life.

The month had its share of disappointments too. I was forced to resign from the International MUN conference in Jordan for the semester. Ms. Ramone had insisted on my presence in the Advisory Council. To catch up with my studies for my AP classes, I had to reject the offer. She was disappointed, but acknowledged my situation. KAS was planning for a secondary MUN conference, the following semester, within its community. I hoped I could participate in that event.

My search for universities was also coming to a close. I had plans to go to Canada for my higher studies. I had sent in my applications and recommendation letters to the University of Alberta, University of British Columbia, and St. Mary's University. I had to focus on applying for academic scholarships. My decision to study abroad would hinge on my success in obtaining those scholarships. Time would tell. I intended to pursue a career in academia, with a degree in astrophysics, but I still sought a future where I could utilize my talents and abilities apart from science.

Mom and Dad believed that Mr. Wilson was my inspiration. I could easily accept the fact that I'd found astronomy to be a curiously engaging subject since childhood. My questioning nature pushed me toward the choice of such a career; over time, I fell in love with the subject. I cannot deny Mr. Wilson's contribution and efforts to help me achieve the knowledge and confidence I needed to pursue such a profession. At that point in my life, he was my greatest source of motivation.

My recommendation letters were written by Mr. and Mrs. Wilson. As the principal of the school, Mr. Wilson specifically had the responsibility to write recommendation letters for all students in the senior class. He was up to his usual mind games one day when he refused to write a recommendation letter for Hank. Hank couldn't help but stutter, hoping to find a solution to this dilemma, while I laughed watching the scene unfold. Hank hadn't turned in his AP Physics lab reports for at least two weeks. Mr. Wilson was using that as justification for his denial. I knew he was kidding, but I couldn't resist joining in on the joke. It took awhile until Hank realized the truth, and he couldn't resist venting at me, "I'm going to kill you! He nearly gave me a heart attack! How the hell can you side up with him?"

I laughed loudly and replied, "You should have seen the look on your face!"

After that comment, it was clobbering time. He placed me in a chokehold until I apologized.

Besides this entertainment, I always made time to meet up with Rose so we could catch up on our lives. I was also enrolled in AP Calculus. I had pursued first-level AP Calculus AB in tenth grade, and I was completing my final stage of studies in AP Calculus BC.

I studied independently for this course; it was slotted simultaneously with the core math class and involved advanced topics apart from Calculus AB. I had the freedom to study where I wanted, and I initially did so at the library. But once I found out that Rose's biology class was set up right next to our classroom, I decided to stay put. Whenever I had the opportunity, I took turns passing by the biology classroom to chat with Rose.

Calculus came easy to me, partly due to my experience from tenth grade, when I had originally enrolled in Calculus AB. I usually sat at the back of the classroom close to the entrance. It was a small room and my instructor ignored my presence, focusing on the other students instead. I was given weekly reviews and quizzes to make sure I was keeping up to date with my studies. This gave me a lot of flexibility to exercise the time I had on my hands. Rose would walk by the corridor from her classroom, giving me a hand signal whenever she wanted to chat.

Hank was preparing for the AP Calculus AB exam, but unlike me, it was required of him to stay in class the entire hour. He grumbled about how I had the chance to at least meet Rose and Tina (who had a free block period during this time slot) while he had to spend the hour listening to calculus babble. He dozed off in class frequently, as he found calculus boring. With our rotating schedules, math classes were sometimes followed by a lunch break.

Once, Hank and I were stuck in a test that ran overtime into the break. Rose's biology session had just ended; she was standing in the corridor watching me talk to myself as I worked through the problems. She was soon accompanied by Tina. Both girls had their fun at the sight of our struggles to finish the test before the break ended. It took me awhile, but I was able to complete the test successfully and rush outside to chase Rose. By that point, she was making funny gestures and openly laughing at me.

Meanwhile, Hank was given extra time to finish his test. Tina, Rose, and I went to the cafeteria. By the time Hank made it, nearly all the food packages had been sold. He shared Tina's lunch instead. Similar events occurred frequently throughout November as we moved closer to the end of the semester. Tina, Rose, and I had fun on these occasions. Hank usually wasn't of the same opinion.

The International Dinner was approaching. Exams would begin the week after the event. Our social engagements would be constrained. It made me wonder how difficult it would be for the three of us to meet during the exam period.

Despite all the fun, my life at school felt monotonous during this stressful period; I just wanted something dramatic to happen. I got my wish during the first week of December when my confessions with Rose began anew and further truths were revealed.

CHAPTER 7

FIRST SEMESTER ENDS

"A simple gesture is all that is needed to change someone's life. Be it a reassuring smile, an innocent promise, plain laughter, or even unrequited love."

The week of the International Dinner, I was busy reviewing for my semester exams. The AP practice exams had passed smoothly, yet there was little time to spare for procrastination. The core course exams remained. I was relieved to find a short break from studies on the night of the International Dinner. It was hard to believe that it was my final year of high school; we had already completed one semester.

Ms. Lana's class didn't involve an exam, but our final grades were determined by our individual performances with the choir at the International Dinner. It was a successful exposition. I wore a *sherwani*, a long coat-boss jacket fastened with buttons. It is a type of traditional Indian clothing for men. The *sherwani* usually comes just below the knees and is worn with fitting pants, in my case dark jeans. Rino also came in similar attire. A lot of funny things happened that night.

There was a presentation to highlight the school's student body representatives from different countries. Rino and I were caught in an embarrassing situation when we made it to the stage to present our speech. We allowed the audience to settle down before we got started, but the moment Rino spoke into the microphone, the electricity cut and the entire stage was bathed in darkness. I could hear Mr. Wilson's laugh in the crowd as the staff tried to sort out the problem; Rino and I stood like scarecrows on the stage. Flashing cameras didn't belittle the embarrassment, but I was happy enough to have some company in such a unique spotlight.

I had caught hold of Tina and Cindy shortly before our presentation. That was when I understood what Cindy had meant about the surprise she had in store for me at the dinner. It was in gratitude for my help a few days earlier. Cindy had been depressed. She was generally not open about her issues, even with her friends. I respected her privacy, and she was comfortable spending time with me whenever she was agitated. I didn't know anything about what she was dealing with, but I wanted to cheer her up. I offered to write her a poem if she would lighten up. After a little thinking, I was able to work something out.

Someone I Like

I like someone.
I like someone who is there for me,
I like someone who hears me out,
I like someone who is there to help,
I like someone who is honest,
I like someone who is willing to listen,
I like someone who is ready to give time,
I like someone who understands,
I like someone who accepts me as I am,
I like someone who values my opinion,
I like someone who supports me,
I like someone who knows me truly,
I like someone who loves me as a dear friend.
Then, one day, I had a doubt, a question,
If I had someone like this,
And that one day, I searched for this someone,
This someone I like.

I searched, searched, and searched,
I searched through my thoughts,
I searched in my memories,
I searched in my mind,
I searched in every person,
I searched in my life,
I searched, searched, and searched
And couldn't find.
But then, I realized I had forgotten to search in one place;
I had forgotten to search my heart,
And so I took a peek, and I searched,
I searched in my heart,
And I found this someone I like,
And this someone I like
Is you.

I presented the poem to her after a Student Community Services meeting. It seemed she hadn't taken me seriously about the offer and was delightfully surprised.

I said, "Are you still glum? Come on. Cheer up! I thought you'd been fine after our talk yesterday."

"No. Frankly, I just can't deal with this. I really wanted to skip today's meeting. I'm not in the right mind-set. Let's just not talk about it," she said.

"I have an appointment with the counselor now, but I wasn't joking when I made you that offer yesterday. Here you go!" I handed her the poem. I could see the joy on her face when she realized what it was.

"I knew it. I love you! A poem! I will read it right away!"

"It's much better to see you smiling! Toodles!"

I received an official review on the poem during French class after my appointment with the counselor. As I entered the classroom, I was met with a warm hug from Cindy. Mark stood in the background smiling like a pastor. Judging from her reaction, I knew that I had succeeded.

"You know what? I owe you one for this. I'll surprise you at the International Dinner," she said.

When we first met, I had given Cindy the nickname "Goldilocks" for her naturally frizzy, curly hair.

On the night of the dinner, before I took the stage with Rino, Cindy came in for a picture along with Tina, Carlos, and a few friends. Tina's dress made her look like an angel, and I jokingly remarked that no one could change the sly devil she truly was. Cindy followed her lead, but she didn't look like Goldilocks. For the first time in three years, she had straightened her hair! She looked beautiful. Carlos had a bemused expression. He grudgingly accepted the fact that this surprise was for me and not for him. Cindy called it "boyfriend ego."

The only downside for that night: I didn't catch sight of Rose at all! The dinner finished at eleven. Mom and Dad used the event as an opportunity to invite Mr. and Mrs. Wilson for dinner during the winter vacation. Last minute farewells were given as we all returned home for the night. Only a few more exams stood between us and the eternal bliss of winter break.

The weekend flew by in a haze of exam reviews and last-minute preparations. My exam list included: French Language and Comprehension, English Literature, Comparative Government, Discrete Mathematics, and a retesting of an AP Physics quiz from earlier in the semester.

Exam week was organized as a series of half days. Exams would begin at eight and would last up to one and a half hours. A student with only one exam on a particular day was allowed to return home at ten. The maximum number of exams on any given day was two. Students who had two exams for the day were allowed to leave school in the afternoon.

Monday began with the French Language and Comprehension exam. Cindy and I were tested on a comparably advanced level. The exam was reasonably difficult. The following day, we were happy to hear that we had aced the exam.

I didn't break a sweat on my exams for English Literature or Comparative Government on Tuesday. Mrs. Wilson and Ms. Ramone had been my teachers for the past four years. I knew the format and layout of their exams. Consequently, my reviews for the two courses mainly involved glossing over my class notes and essays. As expected, the English Literature exam involved a mix of questions on the philosophies and arguments of existentialism in *Hamlet.* On the other hand, the Comparative Government exam involved analyses of current events and political simulations. Due to my experience at MUN and my daily foray into philosophy with Mark and Kevin, I felt at ease in both exams.

My primary concerns for the week had been the AP Physics retest and the Discrete Math exam. The two exams were set for the same day. My teacher for Discrete Mathematics was also the head of the IT department at school. Being the only student to take the course, I was allowed to learn the subject at my own pace. The course topics included logic, set theory, and other "discrete" studies that were new to me. I enjoyed the subject; it was unique in contrast to my general math courses at KAS. Assignments were a test of my knowledge and performance; they persuaded me to think in a logical, intuitive manner. This was in stark contrast to the formulaic approach of calculus. At times, it also felt like overkill.

I felt stressed in having to cope with simultaneous studies for the two exams and was relieved to receive an e-mail from my teacher notifying that the exam for Discrete Mathematics had been postponed until Thursday. The AP Physics retest was inadvertently scheduled on Wednesday in the same time slot as the General Physics exam. Due to this, Rino and a few of my other AP Physics classmates had to wait until the second block of exams. The waiting brought further anxiety and nervousness. Little did I know that I would get beset by a bigger surprise from Rose that evening.

Mr. Wilson often placed heavy emphasis on conceptual problems.

Tests were set to be easier than the assignments. About five of my classmates were taking the retest. During the exam, Mr. Wilson went on an errand to the administration building, entrusting us to not be mischievous. My classmates and I respected Mr. Wilson, and none of us considered cheating during his brief departure. I finished the test at least twenty minutes before the end of the period. I spent my time checking my solutions for minute mistakes. For people like me, who often thought big, my mistakes were usually of a larger magnitude, mainly due to silly assumptions. I was proven right once again on this occasion. Meanwhile, my classmates were dealing with their own frustrations on the exam.

Hank, in particular, was a sight to see. His forehead was touching the paper. From a distance, one could easily mistake him for being asleep! He had a tough time studying for this test with the additional requirement of completing his lab reports.

He had called me in desperation a few days earlier, saying, "Please send me copies of your lab reports so I can at least use your results for comparison—or I will be toast!"

I had offered him the copies he needed, but in his current state, it was obvious that he hadn't succeeded in completing the reports. After handing in our tests, we were provided with a study plan and supplementary assignments for the winter break. This was to maintain the agenda in order to complete the course package and be prepared for the official AP exams, arriving from the United States at the end of the second semester.

We were done for the day, but I intended to stay at school till two. Elementary and middle school classes continued until the end of the week. I had the responsibility of bringing Annie home safely. Rose also had a younger brother in middle school, and I could safely assume that she was staying for the evening.

I decided to wait by the cafeteria in the hopes of meeting her. I was kept company by Rino and Hank who were discussing their answers to the physics test. The arrival of Tina and Rose brought an end to Hank's conversation with Rino. While Tina and Hank began socializing on one side, Rose and I sat by the cafeteria benches.

We began with our usual pranks as we teased each other and gave updates on our exams. After a while, our conversation trailed toward silence. It didn't feel awkward; in the beautiful weather, we were relaxed and immersed in the natural tranquility of our environment. Eventually, I asked Rose about how she had felt writing the poem—and the source of the betrayals she had experienced. A few more minutes passed in silence, and I was close to avoiding any further talk on this subject, when Rose began talking.

Her reluctance was noticeable, but slowly she began sharing her story with me. I remained quiet and attentive to her words the entire time. Through her words, I could grasp the various similarities in our lives. I expressed my difficulties in writing *Thoughts within a Silence* when I practically knew nothing about her outside the circle of our friendship. She wasn't surprised by my remarks and kept smiling.

On a whim, I said, "Rose, I may be nothing more than a normal friend to you, but to me, you are a special person. By the end of the year, I bet there will come a day when you will share with me all that you have kept hidden from me today. You've always mentioned how you could never be open with others about your personal life out of fear of getting hurt and betrayed. I've only received beautiful, enigmatic, and a tad annoying smiles whenever I asked you these questions, but I'm certain that one day you will tell me the whole story. At least, I hope so, before we part ways." These words would foreshadow the start of a unique experience in my life.

Rose insisted that it would be hard for her to share her personal truths, but I was confident. In order to change the sudden focus of our discussion, she asked me about my life. I didn't mind sharing my memories with Rose. At that moment, it felt as if I had nothing to lose—and that I could safely share my personal feelings with her. I also felt that it would motivate her to do the same with me. I described my exodus from Egypt and my three years in Sudan. Several aspects of my life caught her by surprise. By the end of the day, she conceded that our histories were similar. Our conversation gave us a sense of closure and made us aware of how little we knew about each other. Yet, we were so close in our friendship. I was hoping that Rose finally understood the uniqueness of our friendship and how special she was to me.

"So, have you gotten past all these experiences? I can't believe that you, out of all people, who have such an optimistic personality, actually encountered so many problems," said Rose.

"Well, Rose, this is me. I can't deny that. Like you, I'm an introvert. I've only shared my stories with a select number of friends. Even Tina only knows a small margin of what I have shared with you. Apart from you, only Kevin, Mark, and Cindy know my entire history. Personally, my greatest obstacle has been in overcoming my infatuation for Rigel. It was a struggle. I needed something to keep those memories away so I didn't lose myself in my failures of the past. I was lucky enough to meet you for that, Rose. You, Tina, Hank, and our friendship—all of it changed my life. You may not have realized, but you sometimes made me see there was more to life through your attitude and your words. This is why I believe I have an innate responsibility to help you out with your struggles. It is also why I'm persistent about learning more about who you are. I believe that one day you'll willingly share your story with me. On that day, I won't refrain from saying I told you so."

Silence enveloped us once more. It allowed us to think about all that we had said to each other. My mind drifted to my inner thoughts, but my eyes were locked on Rose. Even in my company, it felt as if she was enjoying the privacy of her own space. I didn't know what she was thinking, but I wished I did.

Hank and Tina joined us after their walk around the school. We were all staying in Sudan during the winter break, but it would be nearly impossible to meet. My transportation service ran only on school days and under special circumstances or for festivals. Rose and Hank would be busy with family preparations for Christmas. Tina's family never really let her out to socialize. Under these situations, we knew that we wouldn't be seeing each other for a while.

The Discrete Mathematics exam was set for the following day, but my mind wasn't bent on studying that evening. I thought intently about my conversation with Rose. I had revealed a lot to her—not to mention the promises I had made. It made me wonder if my words could ever become reality.

* * *

Tina and Rose weren't at school the following day. They had completed their semester exams. I had no clue that Hank still had to submit his labs and was surprised to see him at the school library where I was to complete my Discrete Mathematics exam. The exam consisted of a series of logical proof problems. I was not proficient with proofs, but my mind usually clicked under moments of stress or desperation. Somehow I was able to solve all the questions.

Once I was done, I helped Hank finish his lab reports. His offer of gratitude was a bag of popcorn from the cafeteria. The IT professor asked me to stay in school so she could finish grading my exam. We also received our grades on the physics retest from Mr. Wilson, when Hank turned in his lab reports. After all was said and done, first semester was over.

Hank decided to keep me company until I could get the results of my exam. It felt like the end of eleventh grade all over again—except it had a positive hint to it. We alternated between playing basketball and chilling in the laboratory. The IT professor caught us by the cafeteria benches later that evening. I had passed exceptionally, but I was reprimanded for my unorthodox methods. It was one of those few instances where Hank had the chance to laugh at me, and I let him relish the moment. My results were right, but ultimately I hadn't followed the rules. What was I to say to that? I never followed rules. Either way, I received an A- as my final grade. Hank and I spent the rest of the afternoon hanging out in the cafeteria. Wishing each other well for the vacation, we eventually took our respective rides home at two, after I picked up Annie from her class.

First semester was finally over. Months had passed in a blink. Caught in the daily rituals and excitement of our own lives, my friends and I had been unconscious to time's passing. Winter break held wonderful prospects on joyful activities with my family for Christmas. I still had a long way to go with my promise to Rose, and I couldn't say for certain if I could fulfill those wishes before graduation. I would have to make the best of the days to come. In the meantime, I just wanted to relax and enjoy the break with my loving family.

CHAPTER 8

I'LL ALWAYS LOVE YOU

"Remember, son, family is everything. Love them as much as they love you and, no matter where you are, you'll never be lonely."

KAS called it a winter break. I called it sarcasm. Winter in Sudan had an African touch to it. There was no snow, no cold, and temperatures would possibly dip to a minimum of 30 degrees Celsius at night. That was all. We were happy to have any fluctuation from the average temperature range of 45–50 degrees Celsius; combine this with the weekly desert storms, and we have the perfect representation of Tatooine on Earth. On rare occasions during the season, we would welcome rainy weather. The rain helped clear the skies, giving us the opportunity to distinguish the night sky, aside from the pollution in the air.

At night, I enjoyed spending time on our apartment's balcony. When weather permitted, I was able to use the "Starry Night" program on our home computer to track stars or trace out constellations in the sky. Observing the night sky and the stars helped me communicate with my philosophical persona. In fact, that's what got me started with astrophysics. Once I realized the frailty and brevity of human existence in this large universe, I couldn't wait to explore even further. To my scientific mind, there was so much for us to discover in life and in the universe.

Winter break lasted for three weeks; school was to resume in mid-January. I would be a tad busy with the assigned homework and study packs for my AP courses. They'd allow me to be prepared for the official exams in May. Four months were yet to pass, but I had enough experience about how hectic it would be—along with preparations for my graduation and transition to university. So, while merrily anticipating the arrival of Christmas and enjoying my break, I salvaged a few hours to study every day. I loved celebrating Christmas with my family. Even if it was just the four of us, there was always something to look forward to. I was eager to get started on decorating the house with Christmas artifacts and setting up the artificial Christmas tree and the nativity scene.

Time's monotonous continuity was frightening. Only through these repetitive rituals every year did we get a sense of belonging or identity. For Mom and Dad, it meant so much for us to be together during these occasions. During the school year, our attention was diverted to our individual agendas. I would be busy studying, Annie would be procrastinating, Mom would be tending the house, and Dad would be focused on his work. Daily life would pass in a routine manner, and there were only few occasions when we could all be together without our secondary necessities. Winter break was one of them.

I always looked forward to spending quality time with my family. But this year, an additional ingredient of emotion was involved. I was sorely missing Rose, Tina, and Hank. Having interacted with them so closely on a daily basis, it felt new to not see them every day. Was this anxiety a result of the knowledge that I would be leaving the country in a few months? Whatever it was, I decided to fall back on my methods from the summer. I indulged in my memories of the semester. I cherished the memories I had with Rose, Tina, and Hank, but this only aggravated my need to meet my friends. One memory in particular kept me thinking during the break.

It happened during the last few weeks before semester exams had set in.

Tina, Rose, and I were hanging out in the library after school. Hank had to leave earlier that day for a family event. His mother picked him up. Hank was very obedient to his mother. It was a striking contrast with how he was the best brawler in class, often acting impulsively and aversive to orders. But he cowered in front his mother. Tina would incessantly tease Hank about this, commenting that his mother could kick his ass any time, any day. Rose and I fervently supported this view, causing Hank to sulk about this annoying truth.

Tina and I had originally been waiting for Rose in the science laboratory. Mr. Wilson was attending a faculty meeting, and we had been busy playing pranks in the lab with the other students. Had Mr. Wilson caught us, we would have been in a lot of trouble. The laughter reached a fever pitch when I decided to use a pencil and began poking Tina on her neck. Every time I poked Tina, her face practically squished together, and her shoulders hunched up to a point where they could have reached the ceiling. At one point, she nearly fell off the table.

Rose missed the party because of an appointment with the counselor. By the time she arrived, everyone had left. We decided then to relax at the library. Rose didn't know about the pranks we had been playing in the lab, but judging from Tina's blushing pink countenance and my voracious laughter, she knew something funny had happened. Her curiosity led to her downfall, and she became our next victim. We were kicked out by the librarian after Rose fell into a fit of laughter; Tina, and I had desperately tried to maintain the status quo.

Putting aside the laughter and jokes, the day provided an unwelcome insight into Rose's life. Rose had frequently mentioned that her favorite name was "Ace." At first, I believed it was her love for the Japanese anime *One Piece*, but later that evening I found out that it was the nickname for a guy she liked. It shouldn't have mattered to me at all if she had a boyfriend or not, but I couldn't help but feel a bit jealous when I heard about this mysterious Ace.

One moment I was laughing; the next, I felt as if the wind had been knocked out of me. I felt defeated after hearing this news. To make it worse, she seemed to like him a lot. This news piqued my curiosity; I wanted to find out exactly who the guy was. Tina told me later that it was someone Rose had liked in the past. They were currently best friends. I felt better after hearing that. Once things settled down, I realized that my reaction to this news had been ridiculous. Why should I be so concerned about if she had a boyfriend? They seemed to have a history together, but it shouldn't have bothered me.

This memory hit me again and again during the break. I didn't understand why it was such a bother. It was probably because I was missing Rose's company. I wanted to see her again. I also had a promise to keep—the promise I had made to myself when I challenged Rose about sharing her life and personal feelings with me. That could only happen if we were closer friends. I had little time to work with. In the following four months, I had to find a way to get closer to her and make good on this promise. Only then could I know her for the person she truly was.

I spent the vacation immersed in my memories. As far as Mom and Dad were concerned, the same went for my family. My family had a history of ups and downs. I could even call it a family odyssey. I believe every family has one. Christmas and festive occasions served as reminders of the importance of being together and loving each other. But it didn't stop us from rooting for what we felt was missing in the picture. For us, it was the absence of our extended family and relatives in various cities in Tamil Nadu. There were enough problems on both sides of the family that we were secluded; our relatives denied any relationship with us.

As a young boy, I was not aware of the growing rift between my family and my relatives. It was the same for all children. For us, it had always been as simple as giving love and receiving it. As I grew up, I realized that the adult world represented something different altogether. As I grew up, I lost the innocence and naïveté that I had as a young kid. Innocence is a strong attribute of love, a protective emotion. I believe one needs to have a degree of innocence to love. Only then can we let go of our insecurities and be ourselves with our loved ones. It doesn't work that way in the adult world where innocence is perceived as stupidity. I believed, and still do, that everyone deserves a second chance—unless it was too late or it was meaningless for them. Some believed my nature to be forgiving was my weakness, but I considered it a strength and a part of what made me human. These beliefs were tested when I finally came to terms with my relatives' differences. Our testing grounds revolved around Grandpa Antony's death.

I didn't get a chance to know Grandpa Antony well enough. Mom, Dad, Annie, and I left India when I was ten years old. I only had childhood memories of Grandpa Antony, but I venerated the man. He was a wonderful mentor in my childhood, and I looked up to him as a watchful guardian and protector. Grandpa Antony loved me very much, and I was his favorite grandson. This was partly due to Mom being his favorite daughter! Mom had an older brother and sister. She was the youngest on her side of the family.

Given our travels abroad, I would only get a chance to reunite with my grandparents during our annual vacations. My grandparents from Dad's side, Grandpa Manuel and Grandma Sampurna, had passed away before I was born. Grandpa Manuel had died when Dad was a little kid. Dad had three older sisters, but as the youngest and only son, he was the favored child in his family. There was little for him to learn about his father, but he loved his mother dearly. For me, Grandpa Antony's death opened the door to reality on the relationship between my family and our relatives. For Mom and Dad, the exodus had begun when they first fell in love.

Indian culture is conservative. South India still had a society that strongly adhered to its traditional social rites. The influence of such stringent social rules might have lapsed over the years, but during Mom and Dad's era, it was a way of life. India was a blend of two major religions, Hinduism and Islam; Christianity was a minority. But in southern states like Tamil Nadu and Kerala, there was a prominent population of Christians. Both sides of my parents' families were Christian. Dad was also part Sri Lankan; Grandpa Manuel was from Sri Lanka.

Religion was a major element that dictated the lives of Indian families. My family was religious in a sense that we all had an air of piety around us. I was more relaxed in my views of God than my parents, grandparents, and other relatives. I could trace this distinct nature of mine to Grandpa Antony following his own Christian life. He taught me the Bible at a very young age and believed that one didn't have to go to church or fall on all fours every single hour to show dedication to God. He was the wise hermit in the family when it came to religious views. As religion dictates, the elders have a say in establishing the lives of their children, particularly when it comes to marriage. In most Indian families, marriages were arranged by the parents. The parents would choose a man or woman of their liking and have them marry their child. Love marriages were rarely accepted. This was a bit of a problem when Mom and Dad fell in love.

My parents' love odyssey is the sweetest romantic story I've ever heard. It involved everything from a beautiful proposal by the river, multiple adventures of protecting their love from their families, the two unofficial registrar marriages, an official marriage at church, and the hardships they pulled through after being disowned to a certain degree by their families. Today they are a loving husband and wife.

After their marriage, Mom and Dad were separated from their families. Dad still took care of Grandma Sampurna, who at that point had fallen ill, but she persistently disapproved of his marriage. Alone and with little support, my parents faced extreme poverty at a young age. But this experience was fruitful. By facing such extremities, their love grew stronger through the sacrifices they made for each other.

Even though I have heard the story a thousand times, it still feels magical. I can easily relate several romantic Tamil movies and songs to their love story. I often envision it that way. For them, the hardships didn't exist—as long as they had each other. Their love grew with their circumstances. I could easily imagine Dad taking Mom on their first date. He probably swept her off her feet. Dad was that kind of guy. In college, he was a ladies' man. This was obvious when I asked him, in Mom's company, why he fell in love with her.

He said, "At first sight, I knew it was her. It was something that I hadn't felt for any other woman, and it was beautiful. She was fiery and spirited. Mind you, she still is. Her self-confidence was obvious, and she was ready to take a stand for what she wanted. We both needed that. Sometimes I believe it was our circumstances that just brought us together, but at the end of the day, I can't deny the simple reality that I fell for a beautiful, classy, well-read, and sexy woman." Mom was blushing heavily by this point, but she didn't hesitate to give Dad a well-deserved kiss.

Grandma Sampurna passed away during the year of my birth. Dad had three elder siblings, but they had never really cared for him. At the end of the day, they had their own families to tend to and reputations to maintain; Dad was left alone. The sadness that followed Grandma Sampurna's demise was accompanied by the happiness of my birth. That's how my parents described it. My birth won them back the affection of Grandpa Antony and Grandma Mary. During their exile, Grandpa Antony had secretly assisted my parents—although he still bore a grudge with Dad who he felt had robbed him of his daughter. Over the years, Mom and Dad were able to settle down in their own house. It was built on the unoccupied land behind my grandparents' home.

As a young kid, I enjoyed my time with my grandparents. I preferred staying at their place and alternated in returning home for lunch or dinner. Grandpa Antony would escort me to school every day. He was the drill sergeant, and I was his favorite soldier. At that point in my life, things were easy. Under the protective arms of my parents and my grandparents, I didn't worry about anything. I tended to be very inquisitive whenever there were major discussions within the family, but Mom and Dad left me behind with the other children and averted our presence.

My urge to learn about the family didn't diminish as I grew older. After three years in Egypt, we received an unfortunate call about Grandpa Antony's affliction. He had stomach cancer. We rushed home immediately to be with him. I couldn't imagine my world without Grandpa Antony, and the news of his affliction struck me deep. I wasn't one to show my feelings very easily. I hid my grief from the eyes of my parents and Annie, who was just five or six years old, but exceedingly observant and protective of her older brother.

In the two years prior to Grandpa Antony's passing, a series of deaths occurred in my family. When my uncle died, my mom's older sister became a widow. I wasn't able to attend the funeral and stayed in Egypt with Dad. Mom went to assist the family and took Annie for company. Dad arranged everything for my uncle's funeral and took responsibility for all the expenses, directing his instructions for the proceedings from Egypt. The funeral rites were conducted quietly, and life continued. The silence following my uncle's death lasted for several months, and proved fatal. After her husband's death, my aunt and her family moved into our house. Although my uncle bore a grudge against my father, Dad felt that it would be best for my aunt to be with her parents during these difficult times and gladly offered the house to her family.

When we arrived home, I was the first to visit Grandpa Antony by his bed. He was weak and looked like a shadow of his former self. As days passed, several of our relatives mentioned how he became more energetic and happier in our presence. At times, it felt as if he wasn't afflicted by a sickness at all. The family had decided not to tell Grandpa Antony that he had cancer. Grandpa Antony had always taken care of his body, and his health had always been his first priority. The doctors informed my parents that severe depression and a bout of jaundice had struck my grandfather earlier in the year. He was depressed by seeing his eldest daughter as a widow and her diminished interactions in his presence.

My aunt's father-in-law was a controlling personality; ever since her marriage, her interactions with her parents were rare. Even after moving to our house, I learned that she barely interacted with my grandparents—despite them being five minutes away. This truth was more obvious when we returned and Mom and Dad were primarily taking care of Grandpa Antony. I was angered by my aunt's actions and was furious about her carelessness and ignorance. I felt that her ignorance led to Grandpa Antony's death.

There were moments when I felt guilty too. Although we were there, I spent most of my time with my cousins. I didn't like seeing my grandfather in that state. He only had a few more months to live, but I couldn't live with that reality. I slowly distanced myself from him. During a time when he needed me the most, I was only willing to share a few precious moments with him; I still feel guilty for that. I loved him so much, but that same feeling caused me to distance myself from him. I couldn't believe he was going to leave us all behind. It was my closest encounter with death, and I hated it. Not knowing what waited after and leaving everything else behind in life, I couldn't think about such a reality without feeling fear in my heart.

We had to return to Egypt a few months later. On the day of our departure, I knew it wouldn't be possible to see Grandpa Antony again. Within two months of our return, we got news that Grandpa Antony had passed away. I remember being led from the computer lab during my lunch break to the superintendent's office. I was welcomed by a sight that tore my heart apart. Mom was beside herself in grief, while supporting Annie who was crying on her shoulder. I knew what had happened when I was called to the office, and I realized I needed to be strong for Mom's sake. Without hesitation, I walked over and gave her a hug. I felt helpless about how to bear her grief.

Mom didn't want me to attend Grandpa Antony's funeral. She was afraid of how I would react to seeing his burial. I was angry, but I knew she was right. For a few months, I was to stay at the house of one of our family friends. While Mom, Dad, and Annie prepared to return to India, I returned to school. On the way, I gave in to my emotions. I had never cried so much in my life, and the pain in my heart lasted for months. After Grandpa Antony's death, I often wondered if he had known about his affliction all along. If he had, he had been very brave and courageous until the end of his life. I don't know if it would have changed anything if I had gone to his funeral, but I wished with every fiber of my soul that I could have been with him when he passed away.

Dad took over the responsibilities for the funeral and arranged everything. He did everything a son could do for his own father. He once mentioned that, despite their differences, he had great respect for Grandpa Antony.

The family split after his passing. That's how it looked to me. Mom, Dad, Annie, and I were kept at a distance from our relatives. Over the following years, we learned that this was due to jealousy of Dad's success and financial status abroad. Dad would even lose his best friends to this plight. Several events after Grandpa Antony's death widened the rift between us and our relatives. I felt a lot of anger and sometimes despised their actions. It showed me how cruel and unthankful people could be.

Over the course of a few years, my aunt and her family moved out of our house, leaving it in the hands of Grandma Mary. My grandparents' house was renovated. Initially, there had been plans to put my grandparents' house up for sale, but I had strongly opposed the decision. I thought the house would serve well as a memorial to Grandpa Antony. The house's name, Morning Star, serves as an epiphany to Grandpa Antony's continual presence in our family.

Even with these disappointments, I knew my family could never have hope of a reunion without forgiveness and understanding. I had received Grandpa Antony's blessings before his death. Dad also mentioned how, prior to our departure from India, he had a private conversation with Grandpa Antony who had blessed and wished the best for him and Mom in life and marriage. Grandpa Antony had confessed that he had always acknowledged and considered Dad to be his own son. He didn't deny his anger toward losing his daughter, but he had recognized Dad's efforts and love for Mom and the family over the years. I believe that Grandpa Antony's words were influential to why Dad took responsibility for doing the final rites for his funeral. Of course, despite his sacrifices and love for Mom's family, Dad's efforts were not recognized by our relatives.

Not a day passes by when I don't wish Grandpa Antony was here to see the man I have become. I hope he is proud of me. Mom often describes how I'm an embodiment of Dad as well as my grandfather in my demeanor and attitude. I inherited a fair share of Dad's social skills in music, writing, poetry, and his compassionate nature—as well as Grandpa Antony's patience, discipline, and willpower. My views and my personality had been challenged in several cases—not to mention in my experience with Rigel. But I believe I still have a lot to learn.

Over Christmas, I had no one else but Mom, Dad, and Annie to call my family, but that didn't mean we weren't happy. We still had each other, and that's what mattered. I loved the three of them so much, and I wanted to be with them at that moment. I felt a yearning toward reuniting with our relatives in India. I dreamed of all of us being united as one family. It may or may not be possible. There might be pain and further conflicts, but there was hope. I realized that I had my share of responsibilities in making that happen. But for the moment, none of that mattered as I was with Mom, Dad, and Annie; we were going to have a blast for Christmas!

Well, amen to that wish, brother! On Christmas week, I fell sick. Falling sick normally sucks, but to have it happen on the eve of Christmas celebration sucked even more. Despite my sickness, Dad and I set up the artificial Christmas tree and the nativity scene as planned. Mom played cookie master and made all sorts of Christmas sweets. Normally, we would attend sermon on the eve of Christmas, which would last from midnight till four in the morning. But due to my sickness, we decided to stay home.

I had been asleep the entire day on the eve of Christmas, fighting the fever. Rest is always the best medicine, and I needed the sleep. When I woke up at five that evening, the first thing that hit me was the silence in the apartment. I was almost inclined to believe that Mom, Dad, and Annie had gone to the afternoon prayer session. It wouldn't have mattered; I was fine alone. Instead, I found out that they had gone to sleep after preparing everything for the celebrations planned for that night. It took some time, but my nose eventually registered the sweet aroma of food wafting from the kitchen. Like a human version of Garfield, I dragged myself toward the kitchen. I was about to dig my hands into the sweets and cookies Mom had made when Annie caught me from behind.

I nearly screamed my head off. Annie was apparently on guard duty to make sure no cookies were stolen before the celebrations began. I was usually aware of my surroundings, but thanks to the fever, my senses weren't as honed as they were in the past. I hadn't heard Annie sneaking up behind me. She had been relaxing on the couches in the main hall; it was stupid of me to not have seen her. It is also proof of how blind I was of my surroundings, especially when I was in search of food.

Walking back to the main hall despondently, I rested on the couch. The Christmas tree was complete; to my surprise, the star of Bethlehem was hanging outside on our balcony. Dad must have tied it up there earlier. I had refused to do it since I'm scared of heights. We lived on the fourth floor and star-hanging required standing on a chair by a narrow passage of the balcony. Looking down from a ladder was enough to make me dizzy; I wasn't taking any chances. I spent my time resting on the couch while Annie was busy drawing at the table. She looked really cute in her sleeveless, embroidered skirt. Mom was going for an angelic look for her that evening. From where I was sitting, it seemed like she was working on a very tough piece. After completing it, she revealed it to be a picture of the mayor from *Powerpuff Girls*. She had also inherited Dad's skills as an artist.

This peaceful moment eventually broke into a pillow fight when

Annie swung a cushion at me; within a few minutes, it descended to chaos. The adrenaline kept me running. After sleeping the entire day, I didn't feel tired. I was still weak, but Annie wasn't taking it easy on me. I could have easily handled her, but I got smacked on the face three times in a row by a flying pillow she sent my way. After an energy drink and a break, I was up and about. Annie and I decided to make a photo shoot as a surprise for Mom and Dad. We portrayed a comic story about a legendary martial arts champion who had his ass handed to him by a puny girl.

Mom and Dad woke up after a few hours; soon the house was busy and lively with laughter for the midnight feast! We received a surprise call from Grandma Mary close to midnight. She was doing fine, but she was concerned about my health. We refrained from mentioning that we didn't attend the sermon. My grandmother was quite the authority when it came to religious services, and we were not in the mood for a lecture. The night was splendid. Mom's baking was on the spot as usual. I received a cool batch of presents including a huge speaker system, a set of headphones, two new movies, and a wristwatch. Annie was drowning in her own share of presents.

It felt like a perfect portrait of a perfect family as we sat around the Christmas tree that night. We laughed together while Annie playfully choked me by the neck. Dad, with his arms around Mom, watched us with relaxed amusement. We had nothing to worry about that night, and we indulged in each other's love and happiness. It was a wonderful feeling and certainly a merry Christmas!

In that moment, I couldn't help but think, *Mom, Dad, Annie— you are my world, and I'll always love you!*

CHAPTER 9

WE'LL ALWAYS BE FRIENDS

"Everything has its time and soul. Treasure what you have."

After New Year's Eve, a week remained until the start of second semester. I spent the last few days of the break reassessing my goals and accomplishments at KAS on the social and academic scales. I missed my friends, but their absence also gave me a sense of perspective.

Being with my family provided a different sense of comfort and solitude than what I felt with my friends. It was similar to the tranquil atmosphere of the school garden. It helped me contemplate my life. Among the friends I had made over the three years at KAS, few understood my true personality.

For me, everything in life—every moment—was precious. I experienced life to a deeper and greater extent than my peers did. At home, I spent most of my time gazing at the night sky from the balcony or resting on my bed and thinking about whatever crossed my mind. I thought that life without scrutiny is nothing more than speculation, but I worried that I might be wrong. Could it be that life is nothing more than experience? These questions were a burden and suggested the complexity of ideas I faced within the crevices of my mind. I enjoyed the presence of such complexity. I found life to be beautiful at its most complicated levels. My deep-seated personality distanced me from my friends and persuaded me to present myself as a different person in their company. It was my choice to do so.

I had disregarded this outlook when I found the friendship of Kevin, Mark, Hank, and Cindy. At that point in my life, I had yet to meet a person who shared my views and my insight. After three long years, I was lucky to say I met that person in Rose. She shared similar thoughts; at times, she astonished me with truly different viewpoints of life. Thinking along these lines reminded me of the obligations of our friendship. Our last five months would pass by in a blink. My friendship with Rose relied upon our playfulness and very little on our personalities. It was time I became serious about learning her true identity.

I had never gravitated to anyone to such an extent. Something about her drew me toward her. Sometimes I felt it was her hidden personality. At other times, I felt it was just us—and nothing more. The strong feelings extended beyond our friendship. I was afraid of what could happen and had a gut feeling that whatever was to happen would change both of our lives. I knew it would be stupid to ignore these strong feelings. After Rigel, I wanted to be more careful about jumping into pitfalls. But I decided, in my winter solitude, that I was willing to take a risk with Rose.

* * *

Second semester broke the onset of winter solitude. I was eager to see my friends again. School had never been a necessity for me. I saw it as a place to chill with my friends instead of a place to study. The next five months would possibly be my last in Sudan; I wanted to make the best of them. My applications for universities in Canada were pending, but in the worst-case scenario that I couldn't secure a reasonable amount of financial aid, I would return to India for my higher studies.

Back-to-school day was regular protocol. We received our report cards for first semester, and I was happy to have achieved high grades in all my courses. Mr. Wilson recruited me into the programming class arranged by the IT professor. I also earned an extra free block period for independent studies in music with Ms. Lana.

Rose, Tina, and Hank maintained a somber attitude at the beginning of the semester. Winter break didn't seem to have ended for all of us, and I couldn't blame my friends for slacking off in their classes for the first two weeks.

I reminded myself to be alert about what I would experience in the next few months; they would be my last memories with my friends and family in one place. Second semester was already turning out to be eventful, but tough times were ahead. I didn't realize that I would soon be reeling from the biggest shock of my life. Things would fall apart, and I would find myself on the receiving end of the betrayal of two of my closest friends.

I was most eager to begin lessons with Ms. Lana. I always enjoyed her company, and my natural affinity to music helped. Ms. Lana had returned home to the Philippines during the winter break, and I was delighted to hear updates about John. After his departure in tenth grade, John and I had an opportunity to meet the prior year, when I was in eleventh grade.

Things felt different then. John was on his own track, and I was in pursuit of my own life.

We hung out in the music room during lunch. Ms. Lana asked us to sing "I'll Be Right Here Waiting for You" one more time. Singing with John felt like I was doing our performance in tenth grade again. We hadn't lost a beat, and our performance was witness to how time had not passed by for the two of us. Now, I was happy to hear that he was doing well and wished him the best in his endeavors.

Ms. Lana's classroom had an element of peace imbued with it. I felt at home there. No matter what I was struggling with—or if I was confused, depressed, or stressed with schoolwork—sitting in her room, playing the piano, or singing took all my troubles away. As much as Mom and Dad were my personal counsel at home, Ms. Lana was another source of counsel for me at school. We had come a long way as student and teacher since ninth grade, and I hated the reality that I would have to bid her farewell at the end of the year. Ms. Lana had faced an uphill battle against the school's administration in order to establish a successful music course. I had always admired her musical abilities and her wealth of knowledge. The adventures I had in her classes were unforgettable and contributed greatly to my love of music.

For second semester, I had an unexpected companion in my independent music studies with Ms. Lana. Coincidentally, Rino's free block period for the semester was during the same time slot. Rino took this chance to relax and accompany me for my musical sessions. His company closed the void in my musical adventures after John's departure. Rino and I were able to write several compositions together. Ms. Lana often commended us on our synchronization. I couldn't count Rino as a longtime friend, but I was grateful to have gained his friendship before I graduated. Two compositions stood out among the many we made together. Both were compiled as songs; one was cowritten by Annie.

Together We Will Be

I see you every day,
Every step of the way.
You broke into my heart,
Yet we're so far apart.
I watch you by the side.
A love I can't just hide,
The days keep going by.
I just want to cry.
Baby, I can see you.
Baby, I can hear you.
I'll always love you
Until you see
Together we will be.
Together we will be.
And things just keep me by.
I always wonder why.
I want to hold your hands,
Until the end.

You saw me by the day
And left me in the night.
I now can't find my way.
Oh, why don't you stay?
Baby, I can see you.
Baby, I can hear you.
I'll always love you
Until you see
Together we will be.
Together we will be.
The day will come
When you'll take me home
And we'll stay
Together in our place.
For now I will wait
For as long as it takes.
One thing to say,
You'll always be my way.
Baby, I can see you.
Baby, I can hear you.
I'll always love you
Until you see
Together we will be.
Together we will be.

Something Rhymes

Something rhymes
Out in the darkness
And takes me right
In your arms.
I wait along
Till you would find me
To have the kiss

That I want
So we sing together
Out in this night
And hold our hearts
Like stars in the sky.
We stand forever,
Our love so bright,
Together forever,
Like day and night.
We grab this chance,
Look in each other,
And understand
Who we are,
And in the end
We're meant for each other.
Together forever,
Our day's bright,
Memories of the past
Are something of life,
And so we sing together
Out in this night
And hold our hearts
Like stars in the sky.
We stand forever,
Our love so bright,
Together forever,
Like day and night.

"Something Rhymes" is a song I can credit to Annie. I was in a joyous mood one weekend, and I wrote the song. I hadn't played my flute for several years, and I took the opportunity to develop a quick tune. The soft trills and melodies caught the attention of Mom, Dad, and Annie; they hadn't heard me play the flute for a while. They joined me in my room while I played the melodies that resonated in my heart. Eventually, Mom and Dad had to tend to their own work, leaving me with Annie. Every so often, I scribbled down lyrics and notes that came to my mind. Annie's curiosity and persistence led her to help me with the lyrics. She had also inherited the musical gene in the family and had a voracious interest in singing.

After a few hours, the song was complete. I asked Rino to put together the musical accompaniment on the piano. Annie was delighted about her contribution, and I felt it best that she presented the song to Ms. Lana. Ms. Lana commended me for the song during our music session the following week and recommended further work on the composition. She also suggested that I perform the song with Annie to the school. Unfortunately this never happened.

Annie and I felt uncomfortable about singing a love song in front of a public audience as brother and sister. Ms. Lana understood this and asked if I could sing it with one of my friends, but I refused steadfastly. The song was cowritten by Annie. I had a personal deal with her that the song wouldn't be sung by anyone other than us. It sounds like a paradox, but it was the only reason why we refused to perform the song.

"Together We Will Be" is a completely different story. The song came as an inspiration one night when I was thinking of Rose. I was recalling our first meeting and our subsequent friendship throughout the year. On my bed, I dwelled on these thoughts in darkness and silence. It became a nuisance once my mind fixated on the idea of writing a song about us. I had intended to fall asleep, but once the thought crossed my mind, I knew I wouldn't be able to go to sleep unless I completed the song.

That night, I couldn't help but feel irritated that I hadn't made headway in getting closer to Rose. Why did it have to be so difficult to get closer to someone—or have them open up? Soon enough, these feelings engulfed me. Combined with my eagerness to complete the song, I produced the beautiful lyrics. On several occasions that night, I felt like I could hear Rose's laughter in my ears and see her smile in my heart. My rough draft was an utter mess; it was filled with scribbles and scratches of the several epiphanies that inspired me. It took me awhile to decipher my own handwriting and complete the final version. Once I did, I felt an unexplainable happiness in the depths of my heart. Whatever it was, I knew I was feeling something new and special for Rose. I eventually fell asleep early in the morning. I was still humming the melodies to the song as I fell asleep, drowning as I did in Rose's memories. Five hours remained until I had to wake up. The following day was a gong show.

Annie knew I had been up to something when she observed my sleepy stature during breakfast. Had it not been for my elbow balancing my head, I would have probably fallen face-first into my cereal bowl. I was dead tired, but the effort had been worth the beautiful feeling. She eventually figured it out, but she was not impressed.

Younger siblings are often very competitive. I admired that in Annie, but sometimes I felt she scaled her efforts to unnecessary measures. I was her measuring stick in terms of any achievement. She wanted to be better than me in all aspects, and I constantly reminded her that we shared equal talents—and that our individual achievements were unique in their own rights. To compare them was redundant.

As usual, she wouldn't take my advice. She said, "I hate you! I always try to write songs, but my melodies are so crappy."

"Annie! Come on. Don't say that! I've always told you that we are unique. There is no formal perspective of judgment that can be used to say that my song is better than yours—or your music is better than mine. They are both beautiful in their own ways. It's like how I enjoy your singing—no matter how annoying it gets sometimes."

"Stop pulling that philosophy on me, big bro. I would love to kill you, take your brain, and exchange it with mine so I can be as good as you," she replied.

Mom interceded and said, "You are both unique, but if you don't finish your breakfast, I'm going to show you my unique methods of persuasion."

Annie and I weren't taking any chances on that. I was still laughing at our argument. Annie's cuteness was irresistible, and I loved that about her.

* * *

Aside from my wonderful life at home with my family, I had a list of objectives for the semester. I had to prepare for my AP examinations in May. I hadn't made any prominent effort so far in my preparations for the exams. This was due, in part, to my confidence. Mr. Wilson was an amazing teacher, and I was doing very well in AP Physics. My experience in calculus from tenth grade was an advantage too. It left me no doubt I would perform well on both exams.

Simultaneously, I was wrestling with my desire to spend more time with friends before graduation. I wanted to enjoy the last few months of school and accomplish my goals for Rose. Having to balance my academic requirements and social needs wasn't easy.

My classmates were caught in the same dilemma. Several of us had yet to hear the results of our university applications. Mark intended to pursue higher studies in evolutionary psychology in Canada. Kevin had decided to stay in Sudan. With assistance from his family, he intended to continue his medical studies at the Sudanese military institute. I was proud to see them both achieve the best for themselves. It had been a long journey since our first meeting in ninth grade.

My close friendships with Mark and Kevin had been fruitful. I was glad to help them as much as I could with their academics and social lives. I owed them a favor for helping me recover from my experience with Rigel. If Mrs. Wilson knew our story, she would relate my character to Hamlet, while Mark and Kevin would be Rosencrantz and Guildenstern. I was glad they had put up with my drama in eleventh grade.

I still remembered Kevin's pep talk, before I had confronted Rigel.

"Oh, man. I'm so confused. I want to tell her about how I feel, but my mind goes blank every time I go up to her. It is like somebody just wiped my slate clean. I don't get it, and it doesn't help that she's so pretty. Worse, what if she doesn't agree or feel the same way about me?"

"Bro, chill! There isn't really anything to be confused about here. You like her, and that's what matters. Just go and tell her that. Whatever happens after, we'll take care of it. You better do it soon— or else some other dude might beat you to it. She is one of the most popular girls at school. Even if she doesn't share your feelings, I'd feel better knowing that instead of hanging around with no answer. It's time you stepped up and become a man!"

That had been Kevin's reply to my desperate tirade. What happened after is a story well-known. I'd rather steer clear of it. Despite the results of my proposal and ensuing disaster, I owed a great deal to my friends who had helped me out of that nightmare. It still doesn't make sense to me why girls tend to choose idiots over genuinely nice guys. I wonder what goes on in their mind.

When I look back at those memories, I laugh at my blindness and how foolish I was. But, if there was something I learned from my experience with Rigel, it was to accept my flaws and the fallibility of my feelings. My failure in Rigel's case made me question if it was wise to live my life by following my emotions and instincts. Ever since then, I had slowly learned, albeit with much difficulty, to control my feelings and emotions in my interactions with others. I struggled in this objective due to my optimistic and lively personality, which suggested the opposite course of action.

Dad described my feelings for Rigel as a crush, but I consider it another phase of love. I wondered how many phases I would get to see in life. One phase I could completely depend on was the cordial love I found in my family and friends. Mark and Kevin, in particular, were like my brothers. I had been relentless for years in helping them strive for greater dreams. Countless days had been spent in discussions as I assisted them in their studies. It felt weird to see them become so independent.

Several of my professors acknowledged the influence and support I'd provided for my friends. I'd helped them become better students and promising members of the graduating class of 2009. The three of us shared a dream of meeting one another after we had succeeded in achieving all that we wanted in life. My trust for them was unbreakable. I tried to divide my time evenly among my two friends, while also trying to focus on my friendship with Rose.

Now that we were in our final year, almost all my conversations with Mark and Kevin hinged on our memories. We had certainly matured as disciplined young men, regardless of our record as pranksters. We had once made a practical joke by smoking in Mr. Wilson's lab. In reality, we just rolled up pieces of paper and acted so. From a distance, it made no difference.

We also had an encounter in Som Café. We were hanging out with Hank and Carlos. I'd decided to get some fresh air, as my friends were smoking. I had only taken a few steps outside of the restaurant when I was greeted by Mr. and Mrs. Wilson, Ms. Ramone, and our school superintendent. After a hasty greeting, I rushed back into the café and begged Hank, Mark, and Kevin to stop smoking and drinking. I knew it would be embarrassing for them to be in such a state before the teachers. Unfortunately, the guys wouldn't listen, leading to their demise, with an unfortunate series of coughing episodes once they saw the teachers.

Mark and Kevin also had a rowdy streak outside of school. Several friends and teachers had advised me to be careful in my close friendship with them. But my faith in my friends was unshakeable, and I had never questioned their trust. On these occasions, life would usually throw us a wrench. It certainly did for my friends and me.

It was an extraordinary experience, but it was not a positive one. Our last class for the day was Comparative Government with Ms. Ramone. About fifteen minutes into the lecture, we were interrupted by Mr. Wilson. Pulling Ms. Ramone to the side, Mr. Wilson whispered furiously. I could see Ms. Ramone's complexion change, and I knew that something was up—and it wasn't good. After a few minutes, Mr. Wilson turned around to address our class.

"I'm sorry, everyone, but I have some bad news. Today at lunch, a teacher's laptop was stolen. We've been having issues lately with fraud and stealing on campus. This latest development has brought things to an edge. The laptop contained the teacher's personal data—as well as grades and other academic documents. The superintendent has issued a general checkup of all the students' belongings. I'm ashamed and sad that it has come to this. We're sorry for interrupting your class, but the school will proceed with a routine checkup."

The class was canceled. The evening was filled with rumors and gossip. Mr. Wilson had been very serious. The staff was adamant about catching the thieves. Even the maintenance workers were checked. Each and every student was screened through a security procedure before leaving campus. Mrs. Wilson and Ms. Ramone staunchly proclaimed that the senior class had no role in the theft, but it didn't stop us from being checked.

Kevin and Mark were part Sudanese. They had intricate, friendly relations with the maintenance workers at school. Often I would hear insider stories from them about anything fishy that occurred at school. Under our circumstances, I didn't hesitate to ask if they had any idea who was behind the theft. They initially proclaimed (jokingly) that they knew the thieves very well, but after much insistence, confessed that they had no clue about who was involved in the theft.

Yet, I felt something was wrong. As close friends, I knew their attitudes and could sense the slightest difference in tone. When I asked them questions about the theft, I instinctively felt that they were hiding something from me. I didn't like suspecting my closest friends, but I couldn't deny the feeling either. It was then that I remembered what had happened during lunch.

I had been hanging out with Mark, Kevin, and Cindy. My two

friends had left halfway during the break to go somewhere. They had been very discrete and speculative about what they were going to do, but I had watched them walk toward the high school building and the History, English, and Math classrooms. They returned at the end of the break, but when I asked them about their escapade, they had brushed off my comments with jokes. Something was amiss, and their reluctance to respond to my questions fostered further doubt in my heart.

I hated thinking so, but I began to wonder if Mark and Kevin were responsible for the theft. It was ridiculous. There were no reasons for my assumptions. They were accomplished students and were graduating this year. They wouldn't be stupid enough to pull such a trick. More importantly, they were my friends. I trusted them. But hadn't my blind trust in my friends often hurt me in the end? My inner voice was unrelenting in letting my doubts seep away. While the teachers were in an uproar, I was facing inner struggles about my friends' actions.

If my assumptions were true, I was in a compromising position where I would have to choose between remaining silent or betraying my friends. After class was dismissed, I was led by Mrs. Wilson and our IT professor to stay in Mr. Wilson's lab until my ride arrived. I soon found myself in the company of Rose, Tina and Hank. Annie was also escorted to join our group so she could stay by my side. While Mrs. Wilson conversed with the other teacher, obviously disappointed about the situation, Rose, Tina, Hank, and I passed time as usual. Annie enjoyed being in our company, bouncing with opinions and apparently clueless to the seriousness of what was happening around us.

After an hour, we made it back home. I hadn't heard from Mark and Kevin since we were dismissed from class. I related the day's events to Mom and Dad; they were both astonished. I held back from sharing my suspicions with them, but I was plagued by doubts for the rest of the evening.

* * *

"So, do you have any ideas why two of your classmates aren't in class today?" Mr. Wilson said before General Physics class the following day.

I hadn't noticed Mark and Kevin's absence until that point. This didn't bode well with the results of what had happened. I had heard the ones responsible for the theft were found the prior evening and had been expelled from school. Under these conditions, I couldn't help but feel uncomfortable with Mr. Wilson's question. I was hoping to get a call or message from Mark or Kevin informing me that they would be late to school.

Cindy eventually confronted me about the truth during Ms. Ramone's class later in the morning.

When Ms. Ramone left to the administration building on a short notice, I took my chance and asked Cindy, "So, did you get any messages from Mark or Kevin?"

Cindy ignored my questions. Her reply caught me off guard, "Don't play around. Get your shit together. You know why they are not here as well as I do. How long are you going to deny the truth? Because damn it, I don't want to be the one to break this to you."

"So, it was them. No wonder Mr. Wilson asked me that question."

My heart sank with the reality that oppressed my mind. I could feel the ground give away beneath me. My heart was beating even slower than before. The shock was a little overwhelming—even though I had hinted the truth. I needed some time to digest all of it.

"Cindy, if you don't mind, can I ask a favor of you?"

"What is it?"

"I don't mean to offend you, but I just need some space, so I can just get over this. I'm going to excuse myself from your company for now. Is that okay?"

"All right. I understand, but just don't kill yourself over this. I'm here for you, okay?"

Her words didn't register in my mind. It wasn't possible. How could it be? Mark and Kevin? I felt disgusted. How did they lie to my face like that? I was such a fool. All this time, I had been thinking I had my emotions and feelings under control, but my unwavering faith in my friends had only resulted in a heartbreak. The truth was humiliating and painful—not to me as an individual, but to our friendship. I isolated myself from the company of others during lunch and receded to my fortress of solitude under the tree in the school garden. Every minute seemed an eternity. I couldn't concentrate in my classes following lunch. I just wanted the day to end.

I called Mom after school to tell her everything, but I stumbled to find the right words. "Mom? Hey, it's me. I will be coming home a little late today. I'm sending Annie back earlier."

"Why? What is it? I don't recall you having extra classes after school today. Honey, is something wrong?"

Mom's voice made it harder for me to hold back my emotions. I was on the verge of tears. "No, Mom. Everything's fine. I just have to … um … do something. I've got to go now. Bye!"

Tina, Rose, and Hank kept me company that evening. Cindy had explained everything that had happened to them, but I had no intentions of tagging along. After school, I returned to the school garden. Tina and Rose had been adamant that I stay with them, but Hank understood how I felt and let me go. At least, I had good friends in them. I hoped so. As I lay on the cold grass, memories of Kevin and Mark flashed through my mind. My trust had misled me. The pain and betrayal I felt in my heart was overwhelming. I had given so much in my friendship to those two, and the reality of how they had destroyed that trust in a moment disappointed me.

Their memories persisted in my mind that entire evening. I told Mom and Dad about everything once I returned home. They were shocked, but they understood that I needed to overcome this experience independently. Dad felt it best that I was left alone. Neither of them discussed the issue any further. Annie sensed the changes, but was adamant in keeping me company.

"Annie, this is not the time. I just need some time alone, okay?"

"I understand, but come on. You were good friends with them—"

"Look! I don't need this right now. Just leave me alone!"

"I'm not going anywhere, bro! I love you, and I hate to see you like this. Mom and Dad told me not to disturb you, and I won't. I will be silent, but let me at least be in your company."

By that point, I didn't give a damn. "You're despicable. Do whatever you want."

Annie sat beside me doing her homework while I lay on my bed, stared at the ceiling, and thought about Mark and Kevin. At that moment, life seemed cyclical, like an Ionian wheel; there was one obstacle after another. No matter how hard I tried, I always found myself at the bottom of a pit. I couldn't accept the reality that my dreams and times with two good friends had ended. In one swift motion, our world had been shattered. Why did it have to end like this? Why was it that whoever I loved and trusted the most betrayed me without thought?

My heart had calmed down by the end of the day. What was done was done. I couldn't change the reality of what had happened. Annie had kept me company the entire time. She was now intently working on her assignments. Watching quietly, I realized how unnecessarily harsh I had been with her earlier. It was due time I apologized.

"Annie, I'm—"

"It's all right. Look, whatever it is, it happened. It's time that you start dealing with what you have right now. I know Mark and Kevin were your close friends, and they did a stupid thing. It's up to you to decide how you're going to take this; depending on that, maybe you will be friends with them again. I love you, and I want you to get out of the bitter home as soon as you can. I know you can do it; after all, you're my brother."

As usual, her response was simple and sweet. Smiling, I gave Annie a kiss on the forehead and said, "What would I ever do without you? Thank you, sis."

Sometimes, the young ones are a lot smarter than their elders.

Annie was right. I had to find my way back. In the grand scheme, Mark and Kevin had betrayed me. They had done it for something stupid. I didn't know the reasoning behind their actions, but I still had a choice in how we addressed our future as friends.

Mr. and Mrs. Wilson also called me in for a counseling session. I knew what they wanted to talk about, but I wanted to get through this independently. "Mr. Wilson, I need to go to class."

Mr. Wilson said, "Sit down. We need to talk. I've talked with your teachers, and they're okay with you coming late to class. This is more important than your studies. I took the freedom of asking Mrs. Wilson to be here with us. You won't deny the presence of your mentors, right?"

We talked for about an hour. I explained everything about my friendship with Mark and Kevin. Mr. and Mrs. Wilson's silence helped. "Mr. Wilson, I heard you were the one who questioned them after they were caught. Did they ever tell you why they did it? I mean, they are from rich families. I just don't see the motive behind their actions. I didn't mention this before, but I had suspected their involvement in the theft early on. I'm sorry I didn't tell you."

"It was not your fault. You had to choose between betraying your friends and lying to the officials. As a true friend, you made the right decision and honored your friendship. Your silence was not a mistake. But let me tell you one thing, as wonderful a person as you are, your greatest weakness has always been your overwhelming trust in others. You are too giving, too trusting, and too willing to help everyone. There will come a day in your life when you have to consider your own needs. Keep that in mind; it will serve you well in the future. I'm sure you'll cross paths with Mark and Kevin in the near future. It will be up to you to decide how to honor your friendship with them. That being said, we want to see you back on your feet as soon as possible. We know you can do it."

Mr. Wilson was right. In the blink of an eye, things had changed. I knew I wouldn't be seeing my friends on the graduation podium at the end of the year, but I had the choice to overlook their mistakes and accept their friendship again. To do that, I would need to confront them. I would need to know that they felt as strongly as I did about our friendship. This could happen in the matter of a few days—or in the distant future. Time would tell, but it was easier said than done.

The month passed by quickly. Life took a new turn, and I still found myself struggling to deal with the recent events. I fell into a bout of depression. I was afraid to meet Mark and Kevin again. I was afraid that things would get worse. Following their expulsion, Mark was allowed to return to KAS on a few occasions so he could complete his courses and obtain his graduation certificate. Kevin disappeared altogether. I couldn't contact him, and he dropped all communication with my classmates, including Mark. His actions made me understand how life can change dramatically.

To appease myself, I spent a lot of time with Ms. Lana. Rino accompanied me during countless lunch breaks when we sat in her room, playing the piano and talking about Mark and Kevin's absence. Questions about a possible renewal of our friendship revolved in my mind. I knew I couldn't ask others to make my choices. I had to resolve this issue by myself; how I did it would play a role in the person I would eventually be.

Soon enough, I realized I could never be the judge to another's character. Kevin and Mark were responsible for their own actions. It had resulted in our separation, but the choice had been theirs. I wasn't supposed to feel guilty or depressed because I'd never been responsible for their actions. Once I realized this, I understood that, despite our current circumstances, there was always the possibility of reuniting with my friends in the future. I realized that, despite their faults, I couldn't relinquish our friendship. I couldn't predict the future, but I could be open to what I received. Time would tell.

I found this turn of events unique and frustrating to understand. Friendship, like love, seemed so fluid in its nature. There were no set definitions or aspects, leaving no possibilities for complete comprehension of such bonds, partly due to their ever-changing nature. My friendship with Mark and Kevin had been a bond born out of trust and mutual love, riddling in all aspects as it united our different personalities for one purpose, and that was to share a part of our lives, no matter how short our time together would be. My friendship with them had met a temporary end, but I was hopeful about its renewal in the future. I didn't know when or where that would happen, but I'd have to be happy with what I have for now.

While I was left dealing with these dramatic changes, another friend had begun making strides toward elevating our friendship to the next level. I believe Rose was unaware of this, but her consistent presence and company certainly approved of something new in my life.

CHAPTER 10

RESOLVE

*"Life always presents us with hurdles, and reality
doesn't come without its share of regrets, but you can
always make one hell of a nice story about it."*

Mark and Kevin's departure from KAS stayed with me for days.
I slowly rebuilt my resolve and moved on. It wasn't the first time
I had been betrayed by someone, but this one cut me deep. This
recent event would remain as a blemish on the trust we harbored
for each other in our friendship. They had been there for me when I
needed them most; for that reason alone, I still considered them as
my friends. I hoped they would come to terms with their actions—
wherever they were. Time could help heal these wounds. It could
allow for a renewed friendship in the future. But for now, it was a
parting of the ways.

My inquisitive nature wouldn't let go of these new developments
easily. I had a difficult time living with such a decision without
questioning my action from all possible viewpoints. Was I making
a mistake in my willingness to forgive my friends? Mr. Wilson
had pointed out that my forgiving nature was the greatest flaw in
my personality. I was confused and felt that I was sinking into an
identity crisis.

Rather than isolate myself, I opened up to my friends and family
about my issues. Mom, Dad, and Annie were my foundation; I loved
them with all my heart. They knew me best; despite her age, Annie
was proving to be quite the family therapist. It felt different to open

up to my family about an issue like this. Often, it would just be stuff regarding school or lightheaded arguments about my lifestyle. I threw away my inhibitions and openly confessed my insecurities. The more I shared with my family, the happier I felt. A simple hug and their unconditional love were enough to guide me.

Rose's consistent company also helped. It was easy to share things with her. Most importantly, she was one of the few people who truly listened. The fact that we had several things in common certainly made her the right person to talk to. With her by my side at school, I was able to escape the harsh reality of Mark and Kevin's absence. These moments brought us closer and—without Rose's awareness—allowed me to explore another side of her personality. Until then, my relationship with Rose had been dictated by the happiness we shared in each other's company. But of late, I felt that I was able to appreciate her compassion and concern for me to a greater degree. She made me feel important. Rose's actions, willingness to help, concern, and compassion were a reflection of who she was—and I admired her. She was beautiful in that way.

Soon enough, I was able to regain my footing and gradually started to overcome my indecisions. My family's love and Rose's empathy acted as a buffer and uplifted my heart. I began writing again. The words that had failed me during the crux of Mark and Kevin's betrayal now flowed in my poems. The memories of my two friends lingered, but I had started to move on with a purpose. With the help of my family and Rose, I learned that life was not just about living and being close to your loved ones—it was also about learning to let go when needed.

A month passed. The pressure was on at school work, and the sense of the end to my high school journey grew stronger. I wished time would go slower for all of us. Despite my workload, I intended to focus more on spending time with my friends and family. I had the opportunity to go to Canada for my higher studies, but it would be a challenge to manage my life without my family's guidance. It would keep me apart from the three people I loved the most. The thought was daunting, but my excitement about the opportunity kept my spirits high.

All I had to do was make a final set of beautiful memories before I bid farewell to my family and friends. No matter what, they would always be in my heart and memories. No one could change that. That would have to serve as my strength at the end of the year.

During the second month of the semester, I met Mark when he visited the administration building after school to get his certificates. I had an appointment with the superintendent about my recommendation letters. My primary choices for universities in Canada were the University of Alberta in Edmonton and St. Mary's University in Halifax. Once I entered the building, I was surprised to see Mark waiting by the reception area. While I hesitated, he got up, embraced me, and said, "Hey, bro! Long time, no see!" I was in shock, trying to smile as I shook his hand. The superintendent was dealing with another appointment, so I waited with Mark at the reception.

After a few minutes, he asked, "So, are you applying for universities in Canada?"

"Yes, I am. As of now, I'm betting on U of A and St. Mary's. What about you?"

"Toronto, my friend, I'm going back to my hometown."

"That's good to hear, Mark. Good luck on your applications. Have you heard from Kevin?"

At which point, I was called into the superintendent's office.

Mark offered a hurried response and said, "Kevin hasn't contacted me ever since we left. I hope he is all right. Anyways, it was good to see you again, my friend. I wish you the best in all your endeavors. I'll see you soon as an astrophysicist in the future."

With melancholy and a twinge of regret, I replied, "It was good to see you too, Mark. I hope we do see each other again in the future, my friend. Live your dreams well."

I made my way into the superintendent's office. My mind-set was disrupted after seeing Mark. There hadn't been a lot to say for either of us. Once my appointment concluded, I rushed back to see if he was still there. I was received by an empty room. The receptionist informed me that Mark had left five minutes after I started my appointment. That was the last I saw of my friend. I couldn't predict what happened to Kevin, but I wished him well in my heart.

The class of 2009 felt a little empty after Mark and Kevin's departure. I wondered if any of my classmates cared about what had happened to my two friends. Although I was moving on with my life, I still found it difficult to accept how people did it so easily. Was it just me who put so much effort into everything I cherished? I suppose it is true that ignorance is bliss. I hoped I wouldn't face any further problems during the remainder of the year. I had enough to deal with; I just wanted to be happy with my family and friends. But once again, life had different plans.

Throughout the year, Rina and I continued to meet outside of school. I strictly maintained the truth that I was not dating Rina and denied any assumption of being her boyfriend. Over time, the rumors had subsided—or that's what I believed. Midsemester, I was busy with my preparations for the AP examinations. I had met Rina's family the prior month, when she invited me to a play at KICS. I felt very happy to have a friend from my state who spoke the same language. Tamilians were a rare commodity in Sudan. Rina was to graduate very soon. Students at KICS graduated at least a month ahead of the students at KAS. I couldn't make it to the ceremony, but Rina invited me to attend the after-party.

She had mentioned that her party was to begin at nine o'clock. I accidentally presumed that she meant in the morning. Dressed up in my newly tailored suit and carrying Mom's handpicked gift for Rina—a beautiful pearl necklace from India—I went over to KICS. I was met with an empty school campus, and the guard told me that the party was at night. Mom and Annie wouldn't stop laughing when I returned home and told them about what had happened. My blunder was a bad omen for the evening.

Lynn and several others at KAS also had friends graduating from

KICS. They had also been invited to the after-party. The party was to continue past midnight. Lynn and I had an AP Physics practice exam the following day. Mom wasn't too keen on letting me go for the night. I asked Lynn to inform Rina that I was going to miss the event. It turned out be a lucky call; Lynn wouldn't take my answer. With persistence, she asked me to hand the phone to Mom. Within a few minutes, Lynn had convinced her to let me attend the party. I don't know how she did it, but I made a mental note to get some tips from her later that night.

I was picked up by two of my friends at a nearby restaurant. Caught in traffic, we arrived twenty minutes late. There were a lot of people, and it took me awhile to find Rina in the crowd.

I eventually caught sight of her on the dance floor. Joining her in the dance, I whispered into her ear about the gift I had to present her. We made our way out and settled on a couch in the student lounge by the entrance. The disco music in the hall contrasted with the relaxing piano music in the lounge. The lounge was set up in the open by a terrace that overlooked the campus; it was connected by a small tunnel to the party hall's reception. The open-air view maintained a beautiful atmosphere, and the moonlit scenery captured the moment.

Rina was surprised and pleased with the gift. Mom certainly knew her taste. I helped tie the necklace around her neck and didn't hesitate from commenting about how stunning it looked on her. The lounge was relatively vacant; a few students walked in and out. It was ideal to have good conversation away from the blaring music. Things seemed to be going fine, and I was enjoying my time as I helped myself to some drinks.

That was when Rina said, "I have to ask you something. I didn't want to ask you this tonight, but I know we won't be meeting each other any time after my graduation, so I wanted to clear the air. I heard from some of my friends that you went around school saying to people that we were dating and are in a relationship. Is this true? I thought I told you not to go around saying stuff like that. Remember the promise? Whatever your motive was, what do you have to say to me now?"

She said this so casually that I was taken aback and couldn't reply. It felt as if I had been slapped in the face, but I remained calm and regained my composure.

"No! Who told you this? More importantly, why would you believe such a rumor? You knew that word went around after our first meeting at Tutti House. I tried my best to quell the rumor at KAS, but I can see now it made its way to KICS. You know very well that I consider you a friend. I certainly don't presume to have any other feelings for you. For you to even think that I was responsible and now to question me like this on this occasion, what were you thinking? Whoever told you this is just playing you."

Rina, maintaining her speculative tone, replied, "Oh, okay then. I just wanted to clear things up. That's all. As long as we are on the same page, that's good for me. Now you enjoy the arrangements; I have to go meet up with some of my friends. I'll catch you later, okay?"

For me, the night was over after that conversation. Inside, I was frustrated by this development. I wanted to figure out who had started the rumor. Lynn kept me company while Rina chatted with her friends. I knew I couldn't leave; it would be plainly obvious that I was feeling sour about what had happened. I indulged in Lynn's laughter, but I was seething inside. It sucked to have a friend question my trust—or I was just an emotional wreck. Whatever it was, I didn't give a horse's ass about anyone else for the rest of the night. I spent some time texting Tina; she began to wonder why I wasn't enjoying the party. Even Lynn had her suspicions. My mood was certainly transparent to my closest friends.

Close to midnight, I bid farewell to Rina and returned home. I was bummed out about what had happened at the party. Maybe I shouldn't have attended at all. I considered Rina a good friend, but her doubts showed that I still had a long way to go to be considered *her* friend. These instances kept reminding me of how Mr. Wilson had been right about the flaws in my personality. By the time I went to bed, the only thing I wanted to do was find the person responsible for the rumor and bash his or her head through a wall.

I met Lynn, Hank, and Tina at school the following day. Tina had her own AP practice exam. It was a good thing that I had prepared for my exam a week earlier. It was divided into two parts: a multiple choice section and a comprehensive section. We had a total of three hours for the exam. After an hour and a half, we were relieved for a fifteen-minute break. I couldn't focus during the exam—partly due to my experience the prior night. I had an easier time with the comprehensive section and was confident about getting a good result. It was imperative that I did so. It would keep me motivated for the real exam in a month.

After finishing the practice exam, I waited for my friends by the school entrance. It was a hot day, and the warm winds of the afternoon kept me company. It was the weekend, and all the other buildings were closed.

Mr. Wilson left immediately after collecting our exams. Several of my classmates also hitched their respective rides. This left me waiting with Dan, Tina, and Lynn. Lynn was her usual happy self. But my sulky attitude didn't go unnoticed. Approaching my side, she asked, "Hey! How did the exam go?"

I replied monotonously, "It went fine. How about you?"

"Okay. Spit it out. What happened last night at the party between you and Rina? I can easily interpret your mood right now. Did you think I wouldn't notice? Come on. Tell me."

I smiled at Lynn's heated response. I guess I never was great when it came to lying or passing up on my friends.

I explained everything, and she quietly absorbed the information.

"I don't want to be perceived as an emotionally explosive guy, but it hurts when people constantly doubt my friendship. I had enough dealing with the circumstances of Mark and Kevin's actions. I'm not worried about anything in particular. I gave Rina the answers she wanted. I'm just frustrated with the people who are spreading the rumors and wish I could confront them."

"I'm sorry to hear the party didn't go well for you. This might be a redundant comment, but I hope you're feeling better."

"I'm okay. Don't worry. It isn't the first time this has happened. In fact, I think I'm getting pretty good at dealing with these situations," I replied with a laugh.

"Don't talk like that. It makes me feel useless. Do you have any idea who would spread such a rumor?" asked Lynn.

"You know what? I don't really care anymore. Whoever it was, I sorted things out with Rina—and that's what matters. Look, I don't want you feeling down because I'm being a worrywart. Let's just enjoy the day!"

We remained quiet for a few minutes until Tina joined our company. Dan's car passed by the entrance, and we waved good-bye. I didn't stop Lynn from relating the story to Tina. She was furious. Hank wasn't there for the sight. To cheer me up, Lynn and Tina gave me a group hug. We stayed in school for another two hours until we were picked up by our drivers.

On my way home, I listened to "Perfect" by Burn Season. I loved the song for its soft harmony, and I relaxed in the car, letting my thoughts drift. The fact that my friends could doubt my trust and friendship bothered me. I supposed it meant they didn't know me well enough. If I had been in Rina's position, I would have arrived at the same conclusion. It wasn't really her fault at all. Judging her under such circumstances wasn't justified. It didn't comply with her emotions or beliefs. What kind of a friend could I be if I were to keep myself down every time I was hurt by someone else? I had to stop being a worrywart. There were others around the world with worse problems. It was time I opened my eyes to reality and stopped being overly concerned with my own well-being.

With that thought, I was able to smile again. Obstacles only exist if you interpret them that way. I realized I had finally achieved what Rose had mentioned about dealing with my indecisive nature.

She had said, "Sometimes, you gotta take life in its stride. Whatever happens, happens. You can't change that. But you can choose how it influences you. If you understand this, even your greatest challenges will be reduced to nothing."

February passed by in relative bliss. We were well into the first week of March when I heard that KAS was planning to hold an MUN conference at the end of the month. Since I wasn't able to join the last Advisory Council for the MUN meeting in Jordan, I didn't hesitate to jump at this opportunity. Tina and Rose also decided to join the MUN team. Within a week, we began preparations for the debate. Time was passing swiftly. Classes would end in April, and then it would be finals and graduation.

Over the next few days, I became occupied with my studies and plans for university. I had received early admission into the University of Alberta and St. Mary's College. My choice would depend on the financial aid I would be provided. My time with friends at school was now restricted to arbitrary breaks. Hank was facing a similar situation as we both had to prepare for our AP and core class examinations the following month.

But it was annoying that each time I found an opportunity to hang out with my friends, something else came up. It was that time of the year; it seemed that it was all building up to something new lingering around the corner.

Things took a wild turn one night when I received a call from Tina.

CHAPTER 11

FAREWELL

"Time may pass from now to then, but memories will always remain."

I received the call from Tina, a few weeks after the AP practice examinations.

Mom and Dad were watching the news. I had a test in the morning and had no intention of being up late. I was having a glass of milk in the kitchen and getting prepared for bed, when I heard my cell phone ring. Wondering who would be calling me so late on a weekday, I was surprised to see Tina's name come up.

"Hey, Tina! What's up, sis?"

From Tina's delayed response and the muffling sound from the receiver, I had a feeling that something was amiss.

"Tina! Is that you? Are you there? You okay?" I realized she was sobbing.

"I'm fine. It's just ... we got news that my grandmother passed away."

I was dumbfounded for a moment. It was shocking. Tina had told me a lot about her grandmother, and I knew about their close bond. I could understand her feelings since I had loved Grandpa Antony the same way. Her grandmother's death was as much as a shock to me as it was to her.

Hesitantly, I said, "Tina? Sis, it will be all right. I'm so sorry. I don't know what to say. I'm so sorry, my dear friend. I know how you're feeling, and we will miss her, but please—"

"I don't know why, but when I got news of her death, the first person I wanted to talk to was you. It felt like you were the right person to talk to."

"Tina, I'm glad that you called me. I'm very sad to hear this, and I can understand your pain and grief. I know how I felt when I lost my grandfather, but I'm here for you, okay? Please realize this. Do not isolate yourself. I love you—and so do Annie, Rose, and Hank. You have all your friends, and we are all here to support you. Do you hear me?"

"Yes, yes, I do. Thank you. It's just so hard to believe that she's gone."

"I know, sis. I would do anything to be there with you right now instead of being on the other side of this call. Stay strong. I know this will be difficult, but I'm sure your grandmother wouldn't want to see you crying. Take all the memories you had with her and embrace them. She lives in them through you. She has not left you behind, okay?"

"Yes, yes. I understand. I think I will talk to you later. I might not be able to make it to school, but I will try my best. Don't tell Hank or Rose about this. I will tell them myself. All right? Bye. Thank you, bro."

I was left hanging with the static. I had never felt more helpless. It hurt me to know that she was crying on the other side of the line. My heart ached for her. I knew the pain too well. It had taken me years to accept Grandpa Antony's death, and I didn't want Tina to go through the same experience. I needed to help her out without making any decisions for her. As a friend—and like her brother—it was my duty to be there for her.

Mom and Dad supported this notion when I told them the news. I hoped that Tina could make it to school the following day. The fact that she had called me first made me happy. It acknowledged our bond—not only as friends, but also as brother and sister.

Sleep didn't come easily that night. I decided to send Tina an e-mail as additional support. I also sent her a poem dedicated in memory of the departed. It took me awhile, but I came up with this.

My dear Tina,

This poem is meant for you—and you only. I cannot describe the despair I felt for the death of a loved one. There have been several deaths in my family during the recent years. We will miss all who have left us. I know the pain and depression I went through firsthand after the passing of my grandfather Antony. He was a mentor and someone who I loved dearly in my life— very much like your grandmother. I know that at school I tease you a lot, and I play around with you in our friendship, but I hope you are aware that I also care for you. Words failed me when we were talking on the phone, which is why I'm writing to you. The poem is not intended to bring further tears. Please don't cry. I realize life will seem a little harder in the next few days, but I promise that I will be there to support you. I hope to see you tomorrow morning, and I hope that tomorrow—more than any other day—I can see you smile again.

(For the) Departed

A pain,
A pain deep inside,
A pain I cannot understand,
A pain that I feel for you,
And a pain that I feel for the love of a departed.
Memories within temptation,
Memories within tears,
Memories within words,
Memories within thoughts,
Memories within a love that will never break apart,
The past remains.
The present lies ahead.
The choice in between
Is what matters instead?

I don't understand it myself,
But I can feel what you are going through.
The pain is something we've experienced together.
The answer is that
Together we can make it through,
The bond that we share,
Brother and Sister,
Friend to Friend.
I'm happy that we came to know each other.
This poem is not a message.
It is not for consolation.
It is for the departed,
And it is for you and me.
Your grief
Reminds me of a past grief,
Memories of a past that comes within my temptation,
Striking my heart once again,
And bringing tears to my eyes.
Words, words, words,
I don't know what to say;
I don't know what to do,
But rest assured
That I will always be beside you.
As night passes,
This today vanishes,
And as the sun rises,
Another tomorrow appears.
I will see you tomorrow,
I will be there for you,
I will stay with you,
And I will help you get through.
Be happy with what you remember,
And live in the joy of the memories.
Wipe your tears for the present,

And give me a smile.
I have nothing to give you,
I have nothing to say,
But I know how I feel,
And that's something nobody can sway.
I will see you tomorrow,
I will be there for you,
I will wait for you,
I will stay with you,
And I will help you get through.
Rest assured, my dear Tina,
I'm always there beside you.

I received a swift response to my e-mail. From her reply, I could see that Tina was well on her way to recovery.

Hey, hey, hey, my smile won't die away 'cause I'm strong, and you know it too. Thanks for being there for me tonight. It helped to cry it out. The poem was wonderful; I really felt your words. You are the best ever. I will see you tomorrow, big brother!

The following day, I waited by the cafeteria, watching the line of cars moving through the parking lot, waiting to console Tina upon her arrival. I didn't mention anything about what had happened to Rose and Hank. I had forced Annie out of her bed early in the morning so we could make it to school on time to see Tina. She was the only person who knew apart from Mom and Dad. Annie was a good girl, and I could trust her to keep quiet.

I soon recognized Tina's car pulling in by the school entrance. Running up to her as she crossed the field, I gave her a hug and said, "How are you doing, sis?"

"I'm fine. You didn't tell anyone, did you? Thanks for the poem, by the way. It was touching, and it made me feel better. You make a great bro," she replied with a smile. I was relieved to see her smile.

"All right, kiddo. Come on. Let's go." I pulled her by the shoulder, and we set off to our classes. The day proceeded better than I had expected. Tina was doing better; she was hiding her struggle, but I knew she could pull through. She eventually broke the news to Hank and Rose who had been a little bewildered by her behavior. I was happy to help Tina in these dire moments. She had made a good decision to come to school. It helped to be in the company of friends. Through this experience, we made a silent promise in our hearts that we would be there for each other—forever and always.

Soon, we were caught up in our preparations for the MUN conference. Unlike the one in eleventh grade, this MUN conference was solely for students within KAS. The introduction and opening speeches were scheduled for a Thursday. The debate would continue into the weekend. This would be Tina and Rose's first MUN experience. Hank and I had no intention of holding anything back during the debates.

Annie and Tina's sister made it to the opening speeches. Mom and Dad also got a chance to meet Tina, Hank, and Rose. It was great fun. I was the United States representative. We were to discuss the Georgian-Russian crisis for the conference; my sole opposition, the Russian delegate, was also one of my good friends. We were staring daggers at each other throughout the debate. Although we acknowledged the fact that our personal opinions on the crisis differed from those of our delegations, we played our roles as opponents pretty well.

I had experience in discussing the Georgian-Russian crisis; we had held several political simulations in Comparative Government, and I had played the role of the Georgian delegation. Annie served as one of the chauffeurs on Friday following the opening ceremony. Hank and I made a pact to move together diplomatically against whatever actions or decisions Rose and Tina's delegations made throughout the conference. Usually, we were the ones receiving the heat, but this was payback. We didn't hold back on our criticisms, and we received a great amount of rebuke and anger from the girls during breaks.

The MUN conference made my studies for the AP examinations a close encounter. Everything seemed to be going too fast. I was sad that my days in Sudan were finally catching up with me. The final exams were soon upon us. Like everyone else, I was working hard to achieve outstanding grades in all my courses. I wanted to go out with a blast. It was necessary so I could present an impressive transcript to university. This meant I had to sacrifice my spare time with friends. It was annoying to miss out on farewell parties and other outings. Time was elusive; as much as I tried to catch it, it slipped through my fingers.

Within a few weeks of the MUN conference, I found myself sitting beside Cindy and my classmates in the front rows of a congregation in the school garden. We were dressed in graduation garb and waiting for our names to be announced. Cindy had just received her graduation certificate and was crying on my shoulder. It was a bittersweet moment. I was eventually called to receive my graduation certificate. It was a few minutes of my life, but they were defining moments. I shook hands with Mr. and Mrs. Wilson and the superintendent on the podium as I received my certificate. I felt happy to have completed high school with flying colors, but I was disappointed that a major part of my life had come to an end.

Like the closing chapters of a book, my time at KAS was over. My adventures in life, however, were just beginning. I was joined on the podium by my classmates to present our graduation speeches. Through it all, I couldn't help but miss Mark and Kevin. I wished more than ever that I would see them again in the future and that we could renew our friendship.

My friends and I had planned on throwing our graduation caps at our professors after the ceremony, but when the moment arrived, none of us had the nerve to do so. We ended up throwing them up into the night sky. Mom and Dad welcomed me lovingly into their arms after the ceremony. Annie couldn't help crying; she ran over to give me a warm hug and a kiss on the cheek. On that night, the memories of four years at KAS whisked through my mind and heart, in recognition of everyone who had influenced a part of my life at the school: teachers, friends, family, and loved ones who were absent.

Rather than indulge in the buffet, I spent my time bidding farewell to several friends and teachers. I struggled to hold back my tears; I knew I would soon be saying good-bye to a place I had called home for four years. I took in everything and etched it in my mind. These memories would serve me well in the future. I was going to miss every bit of my high school experience; it was a large portion of my life in Sudan for the past four years.

I hadn't yet decided where I would pursue my higher studies. The possibilities were still up in the air. I knew I had to dedicate this night to my friends. Mom and Dad realized this too and forbid me to return home any earlier than midnight, providing me ample time to attend the after-party.

After all we had been through, my friends and I had finally made it. For one night, I wanted to lose myself in the ecstasy and happiness of it all. For those of us who were going to leave the country in the following days, it would be our last night together. My family and I were going to India for the summer. I would pursue higher studies in India if I did not secure a good offer to the Canadian universities.

I had no regrets—except one. Caught up in the winding passages of life, I had never gotten the chance to fulfill my promise to Rose. Only a few days earlier, I had been running about asking Lynn, Cindy, Hank, and the others to write farewell messages in my yearbook.

Rose wrote, "I wish we had more time to hang out together. Maybe we could have learned a little more about each other. But I suppose, for now, we'll have to do with the memories we made this year. Most of it was just spent in plain laughter, but at least they personify the happy moments we had together, right? I will miss you. Take care."

Time and life had swept us in their wake; all we had to share in our friendship was laughter and happiness. A part of my heart questioned my feelings for her and the anxiety I felt in having to separate from her. On the other hand, despite not having fulfilled my promises, I felt satisfied with our friendship. Even if I had the chance to rewrite time, I would leave it as it was. Everything at that moment defined who I was—and I was happy.

I had tears in my eyes as I walked home after the party that night. I could already sense a sinking feeling of distance from my friends. I wondered if I would ever see them again. I would miss Rose, Tina, Cindy, Hank, Lynn, Mark, and Kevin. I would miss all my friends. No matter what happened between us in the past, they were my friends—and we had all shared four years of our lives together. Nothing could ever change that.

I knew that I would miss everything in Sudan and at the school: the gardens, the courtyard, the cafeteria benches, the trees, the sandy smell in the air, the touch of the soft grass, the summer heat, the silly moments, the funny memories, the laughter, and company of my friends, teachers, and family. I would miss the fairy tale of a life that I had lived for four years in Sudan—all of it. No matter where I went, I made a promise to myself that I would return to see the city and the school in the future.

I had no clue what the future held. Life had been a great mystery to me for years, but with my friends and family beside me, I couldn't help but find it more simple and beautiful than ever before.

In life, when you bring people together, share your lives together, indulging in their emotions as they do in yours, you risk changing things and losing control. It's all chaos—until you look back and realize that the only thing you can do is record time as it passes so that even when everything around us is in motion, we still have the permanence of memories. Indeed, all was well.

CHAPTER 12

ACCIDENTALLY IN LOVE

"Sometimes there isn't any reason to fall in love—
you simply do. The catch is to know that you have."

After seven hours of traveling, we arrived at Madurai. Stepping out of the airport, I breathed in the fresh air, shielding my eyes from the sun's glare. It felt good to be home. Despite the long travel, I wasn't fatigued, but Mom, Dad, and Annie were a picture in contrast. They were exhausted.

I still found it hard to believe that I had graduated only a few weeks earlier. My memories of Sudan remained strong in my heart. I had spent the entire journey daydreaming about my four years at KAS, and it had felt good. But it was time to get down to business and explore future prospects.

Madurai International Airport was situated in the outskirts of the city. It took us at least an hour to reach home. The familiar winding highways, farms, and trees were replaced by shacks, houses, and buildings when we entered the city. Everything felt different in comparison to Khartoum. Despite the familiarity of the environment, the atmosphere was unexpectedly alienating.

We wanted to surprise Grandma Mary and hadn't informed her of our arrival. After parking by the entrance to our garden, Mom gave me the go-ahead. I walked to the house, rang the bell, and waited eagerly for a response. I speculated that Grandma Mary was either asleep or having lunch. Given the silence permeating the house, I went with the former opinion. Within a few minutes, a somber and sleepy figure approached the front door.

I waved and said, "Grandma Mary!"

Her reactions were incredibly slow, but they were appropriate for her age. She opened the door but had no idea it was me. It was only after I moved in and gave her a hug that she confirmed my identity and laughed in joy. Our surprise was a success! Soon enough, Annie ran through the garden into Grandma Mary's arms. Leaving the two to talk, I went over to help Mom and Dad with the luggage.

It took us a few days to settle down, but there was no hurry. The only disadvantage to surprising Grandma Mary was that we had no food prepared for our arrival. Dad and I ventured to a nearby restaurant to get some food and some delicious Indian delicacies we had missed during our time in Sudan. I also had a chance to revisit Grandpa Antony's house. Walking into the house felt sublime; it was as if I was walking into the past. It felt as if he was still here with all of us. I knew he had been applauding with my family during my graduation. Such a feeling was gratifying, and I took the chance to say a little prayer in his memory.

I was enjoying my time at home: relaxing in the garden, playing with Annie, helping Mom in the kitchen, hanging out with Dad, watching old TV series with Grandma Mary. It felt good to take a break from my studies and spend time with family, but I missed my friends.

I was relieved to have my higher studies at the University of Alberta confirmed. It was still up to debate if I would return with my family to Sudan and proceed to Canada or travel directly to Edmonton from India. The former option would provide me another opportunity to visit a few of my friends—at least the ones who had stayed behind.

To keep my mind attuned to my thoughts and feelings until I headed to university, I decided to begin a journal. It could serve as a beautiful memoir—the perfect way to share and interpret my thoughts and feelings to myself. I could even continue writing it at university. Maybe when I'm old, I will have the chance to happily revisit these memories and reminisce about the good times and changes.

I started the journal by setting up a premise. I presented the farewell letters I had written to Rose, Tina, and Lynn. My final days in Sudan following graduation passed in bliss. I never had the chance to bid farewell to every single one of my friends, but I gave personal letters to Tina, Lynn, and Rose during our final meeting.

All three had influenced my time at KAS. I shared special memories with each of them. I felt it fitting to give them something special before I left. I wrote with heartfelt words about how I would miss their presence, but I also wished them well in their futures.

Rose challenged me during my farewell party at Tina's house, about leaving without saying good-bye to her. I couldn't do so. I cared too much for her—as well as Tina, Lynn, and all my friends who had joined us that night.

For Lynn, I wrote:

Three years have passed in the blink of an eye. Our friendship was a wonderful experience, although this isn't the end. Our current separation foretells a greater beginning and a continuation of our friendship in the future. I've enjoyed my time in Sudan. I met a lot of people, and I found a family among the friends I made in school. Friends come and go. That is how it's been in my life, moving from one country to another. But you are special and will always remain so. Though we will be far apart, our memories together will always keep you close to my heart. I know I screwed up when I forgot your birthday. I hope you will forgive me. In place of a birthday gift, I give you this letter. It might not look special, but the words that I have written in this paper express the feelings of trust, sincerity, gratification, and love that I have felt deeply for you in our friendship. There have been only a select few members of the KAS community who've had an impact on my life. You, needless to say, were one of them, ever since we became friends. I look forward to the day we meet each other again. I will always cherish our memories together. Over the years, I've been counting the days to when I would finally graduate, eager to move on and explore the world. But now, when that moment is here, I feel melancholic about our past. Words cannot express what I feel. As one of my best friends, you were a wonderful source of support in my life. I wish you a prosperous future. I know you will do great.

Friendship is something that cannot be described. It can only be felt. Feelings can never be understood, but they can be shared. Our compassion for each other will remain eternal, just like our friendship. No matter where I am, I will always be there for you. Keep in touch, Lynn, and thank you for being my friend.

For Tina, I wrote:

My dear sister, it's now time for me to leave your company. I never thought the day I met a chauffeur at a MUN debate who was making all sorts of mistakes and hating me with a passion would become one of my closest friends. As sisters sometimes usually are, you were annoying on many occasions. I'm just kidding. I love you with all my heart. I will miss your comforting presence in my upcoming journey. I will keep in touch with you about my life. You better do the same! I promise that I will drop by for your graduation next year. I don't want to miss the opportunity to see you fumble your speech. You've supported me through a lot of things this year, and I don't know what I could do to repay the debt I've amassed in our friendship. Thank you for everything. I haven't met a lot of people who have truly come to understand the person I am. You are one of the very few who have succeeded and, as such, you will always have a special place in my heart. As your brother, my only advice is for you to remain optimistic and enjoy your *life. We've only had a year or so to indulge in this beautiful friendship, but I know that our bond will keep us close despite the distance. I know that it will be lonely for you without Hank. He is a good friend and, knowing both of you, I'm sure you will be fine. Of course, I will keep an eye on the two of you from a distance. Be safe and take care. I wish you the very best for your future. Enjoy twelfth grade! I'll see you soon, but for now, I leave you with these words. They will serve you well. Remember to cherish the past and its memories, live the present, and yearn for the future. I love you, sis. Take care.*

And lastly, for Rose:

One year! Yet it feels like only a day has passed by since we became friends. It was an unexpected friendship, but I have grown to love the bond we share and will always share for each other, no matter where we are. Even now, although I consider myself your friend, there's still a lot that I don't know about you. But that is exactly one of the reasons I tagged along with you during the year. At least we opened up to each other during these final months. I find it difficult to express my feelings to you. Somehow they seem to bypass the amount of words I could use. At the end of it all, I'm very grateful to have garnered your friendship. Despite the fact that I always teased you, I've held great respect and admiration for the person you are. You were right on that day when you mentioned how people sometimes do not realize the potential role they may play in changing another's life dramatically. You have done the same for me. A few days before school ended, I was busy clearing up my room. I ventured upon the poem that you had written to me months earlier and felt an irreplaceable sense of tranquility. Though I wish we could go back to those moments, I'm happy knowing that such memories will never be forgotten. You hide a lot about yourself from others, even your friends, but in those moments we opened up to each other, I found a lot of who I am in you. I wish we had more time to spend together, but for now, I will have to do with the hope of meeting you in the near future, if I make it to Tina's graduation. I'm sure that one day, as I promised, we will acknowledge each other to a greater extent in our friendship. Though this might be patronizing, I wish you to be optimistic, to open up to people, and, of course, live your life the way you want to. You told me those exact words once. It changed my life. Now, I want to repay the favor. Aside from this, I know that my journey through high school has ended. A new episode of my life has just begun, and I find myself upon the crossroads to my future. I will never forget you or our friendship. I hope that, once you graduate, you will take the chance of applying for universities in Canada (if I make it there too). If you can't, just let me know, and I'll come over to wherever you are instead. I will miss your presence and laughter in the upcoming days. Take care. Have a wonderful time in eleventh grade. The year will pass in a matter of minutes. I will be back to see you someday. But until then, farewell, my dear Rose.

These pockets of memories were precious to me, and I kept them close to my heart. Sometimes they gave me the strength to face the uncertainty in life. It was similar to how I felt when I was with Mom, Dad, and Annie. Friendship was sort of like another face of love—and I loved it.

I still remember my last sight in Khartoum. Now in Madurai, everything seemed different. I was clearly taking a step toward my future. After all the years I had been with my family, it was time for me to shine, make my own decisions, and live my life the way I wanted to. It felt daunting to step out of the comforting arms of my family and face life on my own terms. I liked challenges, and I looked forward to a new adventure. Sooner or later, I would have to step up to the task.

For the moment, I could focus on the present and enjoy the

vacation with my family. We didn't know what the future held for us, but it didn't matter. We were happy to be together, and I embraced the love and compassion I felt in their company. On that note, I began my journal.

Madurai, June 9, 2009

It's the usual. Dad's out getting down to business, Mom's at home cooking with Grandma Mary while Annie and I spend our time alternating on the laptop or reading the books we brought for summer vacation. Speaking of books, I've started reading Rainer Maria Rilke's *Letters to a Young Poet.* Just a few pages through, and I can see why Mrs. Wilson lent me the book. I can already identify so many parallels between Rilke's world and the world I currently relate to in my life. I wish I could find a Rilke in me. His words are evocative and thought-provoking.

Life, as usual, remains a complete mystery, but this is exactly what constitutes my craving to be an author, a philosopher, or a better human who understands his self and purpose in this world. I've yet to find a companion, aside from a few friends and my family, who truly understands this side of me. It's like I have my own desolate plane of thought to retreat to, whenever it's necessary.

Night and day, I yearn to find myself back with my friends. Time flows quickly, and I wish I had the ability to see the future. Canada is coming up and with it a new life with new expectations. I feel confident, and I want to prove my success in managing my own life to Mom and Dad. I want to make them proud. Apart from studies, that's my goal.

Madurai, June 13, 2009

The conclusive moments of the day were the best. Mom went to sleep pretty early. Dad, Annie, and I stayed awake past midnight, talking on a mattress spread over the ground. We gave each other insights. Annie was surprisingly shy about our past and present love lives. It felt great to converse with Dad in such a free manner. Dad eventually asked me a thought-provoking question about a girl who I truly liked/loved in high school. His question got me thinking overnight. I wondered if I had found such a person for myself. Dad said it was best to let it come to me. His explanation of love was a wonderful note to end our conversation. "One is truly in love with a person when they feel their absence. Love can also come in the form of absence. It did for me at times, whenever I was away from you, Mom, and our little girl. It is an experience, a feeling beyond and above all others—almost as good as how I feel now falling asleep."

Madurai, June 20, 2009

Eight more days until my birthday! Mom and Dad couldn't have given me a better birthday present than letting me return to Sudan before proceeding to Canada. We are to leave in two or three weeks from Madurai. I've created a list of people I intend to e-mail and contact. Rose surprised me with a long e-mail; it was great to hear from her.

I'm making my way through life as slowly as possible. We recently visited the memorials of Grandpa Antony, Grandpa Manuel, Brother Besky, Uncle Britto, and Grandma Sampurna. The visitation reminded me of the inevitable practicality of mortal life. It was disturbing to think of life as just a simple cycle. You are born with no care, you grow with intelligence, you become an adult, take responsibility, and you grow old and simply pass on. I believe this circle of life, depending on how we choose to live, makes us all unique. I have many dreams. With my studies and future career, it might not be possible to have an easy life in a world manifested by money and corruption. I believe and strive for the notion that one day the world will settle in peace, and I can play a major role in such a change.

Like Rilke said, I found peace in my "aloneness." Life is like a poem, one that I can write forever and one that can change in an instant. In a few months, I must be prepared for the new elements that I might have to add to this poem of my life. When I set out for Canada, it's gonna be fun. Life is filled with small truths, but it's your own responsibility or choice to discover these truths. For me, my truths have been borne out of my questions. The answer may not be important, but by living the question, one has a good chance of finding the answer within. Even then, it may not be the exact answer because there are no absolutes in life; it is all nothing but a relative chance of experience.

Embarking on philosophical journeys has become more and more of a hobby these days. I can attribute it to the peaceful atmosphere at home. For now, I shall end this entry. Lest I'm afraid I will fall into another philosophical conundrum.

Madurai, July 9, 2009

Annie cried tonight. I think the truth that I would be leaving to Canada in a month was slowly sinking in. I sat by her side until she fell asleep. The whole experience was quite humbling. Mom and Dad were off to Kanyakumari, so Annie and I spent time with Grandma Mary. We visited the Meenakshi Amman temple. I felt like an outsider walking amidst the Hindu relics.

The night was bitter with electrical cuts for four hours. Stupid government doesn't deserve the people. Our time in Madurai is coming to an end. More precisely, this will be my last visit to India until I complete my studies. I've enjoyed the break, and there are countless memories to keep. We are set to leave on July 25. I didn't think I would feel disappointed about leaving home, but I do. On the upside, I'll get to meet Tina, Rose, and a few other friends once we return to Sudan. Only two more weeks left. I must make the best of my time with my family here in Madurai.

* * *

Our time in Madurai gave me perspective on the future. I had high hopes for Canada and was confident about attaining success. I wanted to make Mom and Dad proud and take over my responsibilities for the family. The first step toward that would be to learn how to stand on my own two feet without the help of my parents. Canada would have to serve as proving grounds for this.

Despite these objectives, nothing stopped me from enjoying the break. I took endless naps on the rooftop, sitting by the stairs, or gazing at the sky, speculating about future adventures and our return to Sudan. I was thankful to Dad for motivating me on this road. I owed him a lot in being the person he was. I also knew it would be a burden for him to support my education and the rest of the family. I must find a means to support myself at university, at any cost, so I can relieve at least a small part of the burden from Dad's shoulders.

I was glad that this break had provided us several opportunities to interact and build our relationship as father and son—and as good friends. It was painfully ironic that my forthcoming departure to Canada would put a damper on this. Despite all these years with my family, it was at this port of departure that I realized how much I loved each and every one of them. I felt remorse in not comprehending this earlier. I had missed so many opportunities to be with my family by focusing blindly on my studies and my time with friends.

I was relieved of my guilt with the knowledge that they loved me despite my flaws and shortcomings. In those few months, I tried my best to spend time with my family and share my unconditional love for them. When I returned to Khartoum, I had another chance to see my friends. It made it all the more difficult to let go and move on when the time arrived.

Khartoum, July 28, 2009

We safely returned to Khartoum a few days earlier. Our departure from India still resonates freshly in my mind. I spent the last night at Thayalan's house. A childhood friend is something I've always wanted. I believe Thayalan can take that place. It has only been on rare occasions that we were able to meet over the years. I'm happy to still recognize him as a friend despite the distance. We both knew it would be quite a while until we would see each other again. I had a memorable conversation at his house. I hope to see him when I return to India in the future.

Grandma Mary blessed me and wished me success at university. We left in a rickshaw to catch the bus to Chennai. I remember saying to Thaya, while sitting in the rickshaw, "We'll meet. I assure you that. Believe it. But for now, take care, my friend." I intend to be steadfast with my promise and meet him once I'm done with my higher studies. The bus trip to Chennai was marvelous. I couldn't sleep, afflicted with melancholy about leaving Madurai. As we traveled in the highways by the city's outskirts, I beheld a beautiful sight. I had been relaxing my head on the window aisle, not really looking at anything in particular, but at one point when I leaned back on my seat, I caught sight of the beautiful night sky on the countryside.

Stars etched every corner of the night sky. I could even identify a few constellations. It was one of those moments that just struck me. And with a smile, I continued gazing at the sky, lost in thought and eventually fell asleep. After arriving in Chennai, we had a day's rest. The following day, we were on our return flight to Sudan. Our stop in Dubai was short; before we knew it, we had safely landed at the Khartoum International Airport.

As usual, it took awhile to settle in at home. I've been spending the last few days working on my application for a study permit in Canada. I made a call to Rino on the day of our arrival. He was elated to know that we had another chance to meet before I set off to Canada. I believe he also informed Tina about this. She called me that evening, planning for another reunion and maybe another farewell party. She informed me that Hank had made it safely to the United States and would begin university in September. Rose was yet to be informed, but I advised Tina not to reveal anything about my arrival. I wanted to surprise her. I decided I would drop by for a visit to KAS when the new term begins on August 11.

Aside from this, I'm happy to spend this time with my family and friends in Sudan. It's going to be a tearjerker when I leave.

* * *

I was very excited to surprise Rose on August 11. I had strongly advised Rino and Tina not to reveal any information about my arrival to the teachers or my friends. It felt weird driving to school in the morning, knowing that my time at KAS was over. All of a sudden, I felt old. Nevertheless, the sight of the school entrance greeted me with happiness and comfort in my heart.

Annie rushed off to the assembly, and I spent some time walking around. After sending off the driver, I walked over to the garden. It was the same as ever; even though I had graduated only a few months earlier, everything that surrounded me in the school felt like a dream. It felt as if I was walking through a memory. It was surreal.

Smiling to myself, I walked back to the assembly in the main quad. I had only taken a few steps into the crowd, but I was easily recognized by the teachers and the superintendent who were waiting for the students to settle down. They expressed their great pleasure in seeing me again and invited me to hang out for the remainder of the day. I also had official business with the school. I needed to acquire my AP reports to submit at the University of Alberta in order to waive course credits.

Politely excusing myself from the teachers, I waded into the crowd of students. Here and there, I received shouts and waves of recognition. It felt great to be back. Rino and Tina waved at me from the far corner of the quad—the same place I had been standing during the previous year's assembly with Mark, Kevin, and Cindy as we had embarked on our final year of high school. Tina was ecstatic about my return and received me with a warm hug. Rino bowled me over with a hard thump to my shoulder, laughing along with my other friends who became aware of my presence and rushed to greet me.

After the crowd dispersed, I saw her. Rose was standing in the division among the line of friends who had gathered around me. Her complexion expressed surprise and happiness. I slowly walked in her direction, smiling as I embraced her. It was all laughter after that. Rose was delighted to see me and chided my ruthless plan to surprise her, slapping me playfully on the shoulder.

"Hey! Owww! All right. I'm sorry! I'm sorry I didn't let you know. But look—you're happy and I'm happy. The surprise was awesome. You can't deny that. By the way, just to take the heat off my back, Tina and Rino knew about my arrival too," I said, laughing in the background.

"Whatever! You should have told me first! I will talk to Tina and Rino about this later. But you, mister, are in trouble! I was wondering why people were congregating and then to see you—you caught me off guard."

The assembly began with the superintendent's speech. Rose and I retreated to the corner of the crowd so we could continue our conversation. Leaning on the pole, I said, "Okay, I sincerely apologize for surprising you. But, you know what, I was so happy when I got the chance to return to Sudan. I'm happy to see you again, Rosie."

For a while, there was silence. I turned to her side, waiting for a response.

Rose looked up at me for a few seconds, smiled, and said, "I missed you. I was rereading your farewell letter yesterday evening. You always had a way with words. I was in tears by the end of it. Summer wasn't the same. I think the fact that we spent so much time together during the year … I think I got used to it. Then all of a sudden, we had to say good-bye, and you were gone. I didn't think your absence would have such an influence on me. I suppose … yeah, like I said in your yearbook, I wished we had more time to hang out. It's great to see you, and I'm happy you're back—at least for now."

She gave me another smile and returned her attention to the assembly. For one moment, it seemed as if time froze for everyone around—except us. I could hear my heartbeat over the sounds of the assembly. I couldn't turn away from her, and I gazed at her, somewhat with longing. Her words tore me asunder, and I could feel my heart soar. It was an irresistible feeling, slow in its approach, warm in essence, and beautiful in presence. I realized how close we were standing. Her laughter brought me back to reality.

I was shaken for a minute, trying to grasp where I was. Whatever I had felt, it seemed like an eternity to me. Only a minute had passed in reality. I glanced back at Rose with curiosity; it was as if I was seeing her clearly for the first time. She gave me a playful slap on the shoulder, laughed, and said, "What?"

Reeling, I stumbled with my words. "Um … nothing. Nothing at all."

Rose turned her attention back to the assembly. Once in a while, she would periodically turn in my direction and give me a smile.

It hit me then. This girl … I loved her. Without knowing all this time, I had fallen head over heels for this girl. I loved her. I had fallen in love with Rose. Right then, my inner voice said, *Finally, my man, you got it. Well, there you go; you have an answer to Dad's question now. But what are you going to do about it?*

Dad had always told me that you could live a lifetime in a moment. He was right. With one smile and a few words, she had killed me. My initial plan for the day had been to spend time with friends and relax. But now, I was baffled. I spent the day with Rose and Tina. This second farewell would be a little more complicated.

I couldn't focus on my conversations. For some reason, every time Rose laughed, smiled, or gestured, my heart skipped a beat.

By the end of the day, I knew it was for real. I didn't know what I was going to do about this feeling. I didn't know if she felt the same way—but I didn't care. The only thing that mattered was the feeling, and I loved it. On one hand, my inner voice said, *You go get her!* The other said, *Are you crazy?*

Mom, Dad, and Annie took note of my dazed appearance that evening. Returning home also reminded me of the oncoming reality of my departure. What was I going to do about this? The question didn't faze me. It was like a festival in my heart when I told Mom and Dad that night. I said, "You know, I wish I could just stay with you guys or come back to celebrate Diwali or Christmas this year."

Mom said, "What's up with you? Ever since you came back today, you've been smiling and laughing to yourself for no reason. You look like a goof when you do that. You know that, right? Anyways, it doesn't matter. You've chosen to study in Canada; get yourself prepared for that."

Her words broke through my pleasant thoughts and I said, "You don't have to remind me. Right now, I'm feeling pretty good about where I am."

"I think your son is crazy," Mom said.

Dad laughed and said, "What's up, my boy? Something new come up in life?"

I didn't want to tell him the details; for now, whatever I was feeling was only one-sided. I needed to figure out Rose's side of the story. "Yeah, Dad, something like that."

All jokes aside though, Mom was right. I was leaving for Canada in a few weeks, and I had chosen the wrong time to fall in love with a close friend. I listened to "Claire de Lune" in bed. I wanted to talk to someone about this. I certainly wanted to share my feelings with Rose. Her words and laughter rang in my heart. I couldn't forget her smile. I loved her, but there was still the question of whether she truly felt the same way about me.

CHAPTER 13

LOVE AND FRIENDSHIP

"True friendship and true love share one thing in common. They don't presume any expectations and that is what brings two people together. In friendship, this is ratified without action, but love is blind, until someone sees and seals the deal."

Yes, I love Rose. Now, what do I do?

Of all the times I could choose to fall in love with a girl—who I had known for a year and had interacted with on a daily basis—it had to be around the time of my departure. If Annie knew, she would certainly say, "It is such a 'Ross' thing to do," with reference to the character from *Friends*.

But the question remained: Was it possible that Rose felt the same way for me? I had enough things to deal with at home, in preparation for university. Practically, I thought it would be best if I pushed aside my feelings and focused on my departure. But instinctively, I wanted an answer to my question. It felt as if I was falling, once again, into a pit of indecision and confusion—except, in these circumstances, I didn't mind doing so.

* * *

Khartoum, August 13, 2009

I'm starting to get crazy ideas about Rose. I'm certainly head over heels in love with her. The feeling is relentless the moment I wake up till the moment I fall asleep. It even penetrates my dreams! Just a few days earlier, I wrote a poem named "Revelation of a Love" in dedication to the day I realized I had fallen for her. Maybe I should ask her out—or not. Damn it! I don't know what to do! This summer, I'm turning over a new leaf. I spent the evening texting Rose while she was in class. It took awhile, but I succeeded in annoying her once again. She wrote, "I'll kill you the next time you set foot in KAS." Even in her anger, she sounded so sweet!

* * *

It had become difficult to control my feelings over the days. My excitement and anxiety reached a breaking point, and I needed to talk to someone about this. Tina was the only person I knew who was a close friend of Rose, and I brought up my issues with her. I didn't have to utter anything; Tina easily read my mind and said, "It's Rose, right?"

"Yeah. How did you know?"

"Well, it was written all over your face—just kidding. I always felt you two would suit each other. In my mind, that's how our friendship was—with me and Hank and you and her. But I have to say you are an idiot! Do you realize that you're leaving in a month?"

"Yeah, I know. I feel stupid enough already. What do you think I should do, Tina?"

"Difficult to say, but I suggest you share your feelings with her even though you're leaving. At least you'll feel better knowing an answer. I'm sure she feels the same way. You guys are good together. Break it to her as soon as possible, and let me know the good news."

It was easier said than done. Mom's birthday arrived on August 15, and my thoughts deviated from Rose. I wished Mom a happy birthday first thing in the morning. Dad was off to a meeting in the field, and we had decided to begin the official celebrations once he returned. I was preoccupied the rest of the day with my visa applications, but I hung out with Mom in the kitchen. It felt great to spend quality time with her without having to care about assignments or studying. It was also a practice session because she wanted to teach me all her recipes so I could cook for myself at university.

Tina had also arranged a get-together at Rider's Diner for the weekend. I hinted that she had meant for me to use the opportunity to talk to Rose. I had been missing out on all the opportune moments for this week. It wasn't really my fault. Every time I got the chance to talk to Rose, I lost track of time. While she talked with me, I sat there admiring her.

* * *

Khartoum, August 17, 2009

I accompanied Annie for another visit to the school today. These visits have provided me the closure I needed. My departure from Sudan after graduation had been immediate. I am glad that I have a chance now to slowly come to terms with my memories at KAS. I believe I can move on with my future happily once I set off to Canada. Rino and the others teased me about re-enrolling in twelfth grade given my frequent visits to the school.

But today was important for another reason too. I had a wonderful opportunity to talk with Rose. Except, as usual, she did most of the talking—more like I let her. I have been consistently thinking about her the past few days. It was difficult to restrain my usual teasing attitudes and be more serious about sharing how I felt for her. So many moments passed, and sometimes my heart just wanted to speak and tell her I loved her no matter where or when it happened. The more she hung around me, the harder it was to suppress my emotions.

She seemed all right. Sometimes it made me wonder if she knew that I liked her—or if she really liked me back. But then she would fly a smile in my direction, and my doubts were eradicated.

Whatever she felt, I just wanted to know the answer. My greatest opportunity to break things down was after lunch during her free block period. It was perfect. There was no one around; just the two of us sat on a cafeteria bench. I was thinking of how to bring the topic up, but she started speaking instead.

Once Rose began speaking, I couldn't disturb her. She began opening up and expressing her personal feelings about how she felt about our friendship. I was happy to hear that she valued our friendship, and I listened intently, hoping it was going somewhere. Once in a while, I would say something, and she would complete my words. It felt as if we were synchronized. I didn't confess anything to her, but I think it was worth it. At least, it had given me the chance to learn more about her life. At one point, we were interrupted by Annie and her friends; they presumed we were talking like a couple. Although I wished it was true, Rose didn't have any clue I liked her that way.

Yet, there was a troublesome aspect to our conversation. I loved Rose for who she was. She was beautiful, and I wanted to be in her company. The more time I spent with her, the more I fell in love with her. Yet, throughout the conversation, Rose constantly mentioned the trust and happiness she felt in our friendship. She had expressed her surprise about our closeness in our friendship and how she felt comfortable knowing that she could trust me as a close friend. I believe those words halted my approach. Trust—she had mentioned it several times.

Rose, you've left me in doubt about how justified my feelings for you are. Could my falling in love with you be a betrayal of the trust you feel so passionately for me? Have I misinterpreted your words and actions? Damn, I'm confused.

* * *

Once these questions settled in my mind, I realized I had two choices. These choices had been evident ever since the beginning. If I had shared this with Mom, her practicality would have helped me with the possibilities. I had been denying it for so long, but I was hoping it wasn't that way. Either I shared the truth with Rose—or I did not. Either she reciprocated my feelings—or it was a one-sided agenda. This made me nervous. My experience with Rigel had been a complete disaster. I didn't want to mess this one up either, and I wanted the result to be favorable to me.

To make matters worse, I didn't want my friendship with Rose to be ruined because of this. I had seen too many friends and couples go their separate ways due to similar circumstances. At first, things would be uncomfortable, and gradually distance would set in, resulting in mutual isolation. I didn't want to lose my friend, but I wanted to express my love for her.

I was preparing to leave Sudan in a few weeks. To tell her the truth, then, after all this time and leave, there was a high possibility that I could hurt her feelings. It was ironic that the one time I wanted to say I love you to the girl I admired and cared about, the circumstances of our friendship stood in the way. Damn it! Why did this have to happen?

I called Tina in the evening and talked to her about this.

She said, "You're like my brother. Rose is like my best friend. I don't want to see either of you get hurt or emotional because of this. I know that if you decide not to tell her, you will have to live with a question of possibility. I can't say for sure what Rose feels—or how she will react. I know that you are suited for each other, and I would be the happiest person to see the both of you together. Despite the fact that you are leaving to Canada, I know that if you two were in a relationship, you would be able to manage the distance. But at the same time, I can't imagine how she would feel if she thinks of you in a similar way and you leave without saying a word.

"I'm sorry, bro. I'm not really providing you any leverage here. But I'll tell you this, whatever happens, happens. Trust your feelings and choose what you want to do. It's worth the risk to face what might happen later—instead of sitting here speculating about the results. I can see you love her so much, and love isn't bad. Not sharing it is—even if it means loss. Life isn't about planning ahead all the time; sometimes you just have to make the move."

Tina was right, but I felt indecisive. I didn't know what to do. I didn't want to make a decision that would hurt the one I loved. I debated my choices before meeting up with the gang at Rider's Diner on Thursday. My feelings were like a pendulum, replicating the cyclic nature of time. During the day, I would decide to take action and tell Rose the truth, but by night I would withdraw my decision. There was no point in talking to Annie or Tina about this anymore. I needed to do this for myself. I withdrew once again to my isolation.

In one such session, I entertained my thoughts with a poem. "Distance" was about the sense of separation I felt with Rose— bridged by my questions and choices on what to do with my feelings for her.

Distance

Watching you from the distance,
Remaining in your presence,
Ignorant of my absence,
Watching you from the distance.
Passing of a gift,
Our love,
From me
To you.
Receiving of a life,
Ready to love,
I can't say
A feeling beyond my heart's comprehension.
Walking in my mind,
Seeing you in my heart's eye,
An irresistible feeling,
Love of your being.
Wanting of tears,

Embrace our love,
Distant in reality,
Close in our hearts.
Isolated in my tears,
I love you.
Time doesn't exist
In a world where our love persists.
Breathless I remain,
Feelings surmounting in my heart,
Your love descending in my mind,
Your presence remaining by my side.
Something I will never forget,
Something I have never felt,
Someone I need now,
You.
Want to lie down on your lap,
Hold you by the shoulder,
Hug you tightly by my side,
Kiss you on the lips.
Fear of losing you
Consoled in our memories,
Trying to control myself,
Tears I cannot resist.
I love you,
I will love you,
I will always love you,
I love you.
Watching from a distance,
Isolated by distance,
Feelings from a distance,
Love of a distance.
Hands trembling,
Words failing,
Tears falling,

Heart reaching for you.
The third time,
I have cried,
A forgotten reality of love,
A play of life.
Never can I forget
A smile that was given,
A laugh that was provided,
A love that was always kept in us.
Writing from so far away,
Hoping against hope,
Loving against truth,
Falling for you.
Sorrow within,
Mingled with a love,
I have felt;
For days I have ignored, but not anymore.
Missing your presence,
Holding on to your memories,
Life passes by
As I remain waiting.
The day will come,
The truth will be found,
Tears will be shed,
And I will find you by my side.
United once again,
Falling now
To rise later,
A love, eternal and forever.
For you, Rose,
Feelings I have kept hidden,
Feelings I have felt,
Having fallen for you.
In love.

Quite the crowd showed up for our party at Rider's Diner on Thursday, including Tina and her sister, Rose, Rino, and Annie. We had fun until we had to decide who would be paying for the expenses. The event was arranged as a get-together as well as a final farewell for me, so I was off the hook. I was expecting to get my Temporary Resident Visa for Canada the following week. My flight would be the week after.

While the old crowd hung around late into the night, several of my friends left early. Eventually, it was just Annie, Rose, Tina, her sister and me. Rose and I sat together with Annie in the middle. She tormented me with questions, and I tried to evade Tina's piercing glance on every occasion, signaling me to talk to Rose. I had brought my digital camera, and Annie was relentless in taking pictures. I didn't mind this at all and was happy enough to participate in gathering a collection of farewell snapshots with my friends. If things were to proceed as planned, and I received my visa without hassle in a week, it would be difficult to meet my friends again.

While the others passed time in laughter, I realized I wasn't ready to share my feelings with Rose. Be it nervousness or plain old embarrassment, I didn't want to ruin the joyous occasion. Everybody was having fun, and I didn't want to ruin the atmosphere. If it came to it, I would just have to write another farewell letter to Rose before I left. I would try my best to tell her what I wanted—something I failed to do in person.

As the clock hit midnight, it was evident that we were all running low on charge, despite the consistent laughter around the table. Annie was nearly asleep on my shoulder, and we decided to call it a night. Annie and I had to call a taxi for our ride home.

While waiting by the sidewalk, Rose pulled me to a corner and said, "I know that I might not see you again after this, but I do hope you pay one last visit to the school before you leave. I had great fun today. We all just gave in to the laughter. I nearly forgot this was actually your final farewell party. Anyways, don't leave without saying a word, okay? I'll be disappointed if that happens. Pay us a visit at school next week. But, most importantly, you better give me a farewell letter before you set off. You do have one written up, right?"

She said this with such expectation, that—while I was taken aback—I didn't hesitate to reply, "Oh yeah, of course." My heart sank as she gave me a sweet smile and left me hanging while I waited for a taxi.

Aside from failing to share my feelings with Rose, the evening was perfect. The reality of my departure was upon us. Annie and I weren't even lectured for being late. I think Mom and Dad wanted me to enjoy my last few days as much as possible.

I dedicated the rest of the weekend to my family. Not a lot went on. I gambled with Mom and Dad and watched *Big Fish*. The movie's father-son relationship certainly resonated in my heart. I shivered to imagine a reality when I had to return from school and not see Mom, Dad, or Annie. The reminder of my responsibilities and goals, though, motivated me and kept me strong. My daily life was now divided between time with my family and my isolated thoughts on Rose. I wrote a series of poems during these days to highlight my love life.

A Little Pain

Separated by a window of a world,
You and I remain
Looking at each other,
Reflections on an ethereal plane.
I see you on the other side of me
Watching over
A final wave,
And you seem to vanish into the ether.
Taking a step at one turn,
I keep walking,

Wanting to look back,
Knowing you're right behind me.
You said it yourself;
A journey of a thousand miles starts with a single step,
Yet the journey of our friendship
Began with a single step and has now abruptly
stopped after a thousand miles.
Time will pass,
Relatively for you and me,
Not knowing the future;
In my return, we don't know who we will be.
Nevertheless,
Our hearts will remain true.
The promise of our love
Is good enough for proof.
I'm going to miss you,
And I will keep saying that to myself.
Knowing I won't see you smile by my side the next day
Only makes me wish that time will stay.
Every journey has a destination,
But sometimes the journey is the destination.
I know my destination even now,
And I will take this journey, 'cause for me you
are the journey and the destination.
I want you to be happy
In the memories that we have had.
Knowing that there will be more in the future
Is a word that I give you right now.
There are no special moments or times;
It is what one makes of their time
That makes things special.
For me, my time with you was and will be special.
You will remain in my heart,
And I will carry our memories

Though I go alone.
Within me, we remain together and strong.
Shadows of each other
We have been.
Now to leave one another
Is a question that I would have never foreseen.
A little pain
Comes and goes,
But my love for you
Lifts me through.
A last embrace
Is what I ask for,
And a kiss to remember
To make my heart soar.
I will be there for you,
Day by day.
Seek me in your memories,
And you will find me, smiling, in the way.
I know you will be there for me.
Night and night,
I will seek you in my heart
And find you, embracing me, though we are so far apart.
And again a little pain,
I will feel and be happy,
Not at our separation
But at the love that still grows in you and me.
Words shrouded with deep feelings,
Hearts enamored in an eternal love,
Pain embraced in our separation,
Love in your absence felt,
And consolation found in me, where you will always be.

Hold Me Close

Crossing my heart,
I believe
I see you in it,
Though now you remain so far.
As days go by,
I remain
Lost in my way,
My life spent in thoughts.
Having been so close,
And for now,
To watch you from so far,
Something I cannot envision.
Life becomes relative,
And without you
I lie,
Seeking what went past with a soul I can't hide.
Hug me tight,
Love me through,
'Cause without you
My life is at a close.

* * *

Annie and I argued frequently about being honest or dishonest to my feelings for Rose. It only resulted in further confusion. I couldn't predict the future; debating without taking any action was a mistake. If Rose reciprocated my feelings, then great! But if our friendship outweighed my feelings for her, I would still be happy to remain her friend! Maybe it was time I trusted my feelings for Rose. At the same time, I was willing to hear her out and respect her choice—even if the results were unfavorable to me. It would be difficult, but it was the only way.

Rose and I had always been honest with our feelings toward each other in our friendship; if she valued our friendship, I would have to abide by those terms. Writing a letter to her would only be tougher if I told a lie. The greatest obstacle would be making sure that she wouldn't get hurt. I didn't want a rift in our friendship, but I believed the risk was worth it. The greatest mistake I could make would be to not share my love with her. Why did it have to be so difficult to express three simple words and have someone accept them?

I wasn't sure what would happen, but I was set on telling her the truth. At least my letter could speak on my behalf. I was ready to bear the weight of my decision. Plus, I didn't want to be a coward. Life is no fun without risks, and I should have the courage to at least let her know how I felt. I hoped that—no matter the outcome—we could still remain friends.

* * *

The week following our outing at Rider's Diner, my family received news that my visa would be delayed. Due to this, my stay in Sudan was extended until the second week of September. I would miss the first few lectures at university and would have to catch up once I settled down.

I spent the last week of August visiting KAS, taking trips with Annie, and meeting my friends. Things were busy since the students were well into the school year; it was rare that I had a chance to talk to Rose or Tina. I hung out at the library all day, sporadically seeing friends. To make my visits worthwhile, I started writing my farewell letter to Rose during my spare time at the library. I planned to give her a few gifts with the letter—as mementos of our friendship and my love for her. I wanted to share my feelings with her directly, but if that didn't happen, I could write them in a letter.

I found it difficult to express what I felt; I felt apprehension, curiosity, compassion, and love. Sometimes I felt as if I was repeating things, but ultimately I resolved to provide a clear opinion. I realized, while writing the letter, that it was the first time I was proclaiming my love to a girl. When I wrote, "I love you," I experienced a similar feeling to when Rose and I had been at the assembly. With my skills as a poet and a writer, I was surprised to find how difficult it was to express what I felt for her. It was an experience beyond words.

I was giving her the liberty to read the letter when she wanted—I would await her answer patiently. Reminiscing about our time together often makes me smile. Looking back to when we first met, I find it ridiculous that I hadn't fallen for her right then and there. Her smile crossed my mind frequently while I wrote the letter, and I felt as if she was in my presence.

I wondered if Dad felt the same way when he had fallen in love with Mom. On one occasion, I asked him about how he had decided on their future.

He said, "You don't think. You feel."

I replied, "Dad, that's Bruce Lee's dialogue from *Enter the Dragon*."

He said, "So what? It fits!"

My letter was a physical—but slightly diminished—embodiment of my feelings for Rose. For the time being, it would have to do. I hoped that my love in the letter would reflect in her heart.

Annie was adamant that I share the progress of my "love business" with Mom and Dad. But I was equally persistent and maintained absolute silence about the affair. I wanted to hear from Rose first—and that was going to take awhile. Until then, Mom and Dad didn't need to know. I was fine just spending time with my family. Breaking the news about Rose could wait.

* * *

Although my stay in Sudan had been extended, my family was grumpy. Mom, in particular, was having a difficult time. I sympathized with her. She had looked after me and protected me during my childhood. She was doing the same now—even if it meant she had to let me follow my own path. I spent my time at home in her company while Dad was at work and Annie was at school. I had no interest in learning cooking recipes and usually sat at the kitchen table while we talked smack back and forth. I could sense that she was hurting inside, and I felt helpless about making things better.

It was difficult for all of us. I knew I would miss her the most. After all, she was the one who made me the person I am today. She was my guardian in all aspects, and I loved her dearly. I frequently diverted our conversations away from thoughts of my departure, entertaining her with laughter and joy. I wanted her to know that it was only a temporary separation.

My exploits at university were yet to begin, but I was already thinking of my return home. Mom was the heart of our family. She held it together, and I needed her to be strong so that I could be strong. I didn't stop kissing her on the cheek or hugging her at random times. I just wanted her to know that I loved her too.

When I finished my farewell letter to Rose, I sent Tina an e-mail to let her know I had chosen this course of action.

Hey, sis,

I've made my decision. I'll be leaving within a week, but I plan to visit Rose at school one day. I've written her a farewell letter along with some mementos I plan to leave behind. Don't worry; I have some for you too. Anyways, I know things are busy for both of you at school, so I hope I get the chance to talk to her directly about this. If not, I've explained everything in the letter. It's all up to her after that.

It sucks that I'm to leave at this time, and if she says yes, it will be difficult for both of us to hold off the distance. I'm thankful for your support. Your advice was much needed, and it motivated me to take a step forward in this situation. Over the last few visits to KAS, Rose and I have talked a lot. I got the chance to know her a lot better, and she even shared some personal things with me that she hasn't done so with you or her closest friends. I don't mean to say this to make you jealous, but her actions have made me feel very protective of her and also gave me hope that the ultimate result will be favorable to me. Rose always liked me for my honesty. I couldn't write a letter to her knowing that I was writing a lie.

I'm still struggling to keep an open mind about what may happen in the future. If she reciprocates my feelings, I'll be the happiest man in the world. If not, I hope we can still be friends. I feel that I owe this to myself. It would make all the difference if I tell her the truth instead of her finding out from someone else. The terms of our friendship constrained my choices. But I'm going forward with my decision to let her know.

I can't predict how she will react to what I have to say. She might be shocked or even hurt; for some reason, it's possible that a rift may occur in our friendship. I don't want to be a burden to her in any way. Once I leave, you're the only person at school she recognizes as a close friend. You're the only one who can support her. I'm willing to take the weight of my decisions, even if it means I am to lose her friendship. I can't step back now, but knowing her, I have hope that it won't end that way.

Rose acknowledged my friendship, and in my eyes she is a very important person. I care for her and that is why I feel that I deserve to share my feelings with her. At first when I met her, it was her evasive personality that caught my eye. I should have realized then that I had fallen in love with her. Anyways, I want you to be there for her when I can't, to support her, in case things go awry. Please do this for me as a favor for your brother. I ask no more.

Thank you so much for everything. I will miss you. But I know we'll keep in touch. Love you, sis. Take care.

I didn't have to wait long for Tina's reply:

Hey, bro,

I'm not going to be formal about this. You know that you don't need to ask me to be there for her. I will be there for her and you! You are both my closest friends, aside from Hank. I would never stop caring for both of you, well, if it depends on money, I'd prefer you as you're my source of income for lunches at school. Just kidding!

But, jokes aside, seriously, I will be there for her and you. Whatever you do, I'm sure you're doing it for your own good, and things will be fine. I just want to make sure that you don't push yourself away from any of us because of this. We're all in this together. We're all friends. Hank's gone, and I can feel the pain of distance. But that doesn't mean it's all over. We have got to persevere. I hope that the outcome is good, 'cuz I kinda think you are doing the right thing by telling her. God bless you, bro!

I wish you all the best and hope it ends well for the two of you! I can see how much you love her. You're both meant to be together.

Love,
Tina

P.S. Say hi from me to your mom and dad. I've always had a great time talking to them whenever they visit the school! Once again, good luck! You better let me know how things go! Love you!

Tina's soothing words boosted my confidence. During the first week of September, I started packing. Dad had received a call from the embassy informing him that I should receive the visa by the end of the week.

I had a list of things that I wished to take to Canada, ranging from books, albums, clothes, and accessories. While I was busy at home, I got frequent updates from Rose or Tina about school. In one instance, Rose texted me for travel updates, and I assured her I'd pay a visit to school before I left.

I'd collected an assortment of gifts, including a silver chain, along with the poems I'd written for Rose. It might be overkill, but I might as well pull out all the stops. Since we didn't have a printer at home, I e-mailed the letter to Dad as an attachment, requesting him to print it out for me in his office. This also offered me another opportunity to bond with Dad.

Dad had taken note of my farewell letter and, hinting at our previous interactions on this matter, he replied to my e-mail. His compelling, heartfelt message was proof of his never-ending love for me and his understanding personality.

Hi, my son,

I appreciate how much you respect your dad's integrity by sending your personal letters to be printed by me. I respect your trust in me. You are not a child anymore. You are a young man, so I also respect your privacy.

I did not read any of your poems or letters. But as I was printing them, I had a feeling that you were in trouble. I certainly felt you were in an emotional entanglement. Trust me, I did not read any of it.

I only read your instructions. I am amazed at your energy. However, to be honest, I was a bit upset by one fact. You had so much energy to write to someone you found and knew, maybe for a year, or two, I don't know. But you never thought of finding such energy for your father who knows you and has loved you for eighteen years. I'm saying this certainly not to upset you but to make you reflect for a while and help you know yourself better.

I want you to realize two things. First, as a child, I was always alone and made my life on my own. But you are not alone. *You have your father, mother, and sister. I know that you share several things with Annie, and I am pleased with the close bond you two share as brother and sister. Second, until this moment, my whole life and work has been dedicated to our family. Sometimes I buried my dreams for you to accomplish yours. I don't expect you to pay me back or remember me for that. I grew up without a father. But you have me. As such, I can sacrifice my life for you so yours can be better. I do this not based on my love for you, but for the respect I have for you, your determination, and hard work.*

You may or may not disappoint me, but you should not disappoint yourself. Whatever it is, be open with us. There is nothing wrong in sharing, and you know Mom and I are certainly open in the love department. Mom will be practical as usual, but at the end of the day, we all care for you. I promise I didn't read your letter, but I just want you to know that we're all here in case you just want to talk about it.

This is particularly important as you will leave us in a few days. I don't want you to hide anything that causes you discomfort. Sometimes, sharing the burden helps too. I try my best to be there for you, Mom, and Annie—just as you are there for me. We are like a team, so don't be afraid to share things. I know that we don't have much time and I'm always busy in the office, so I'll tell you a few words of advice.

Save your energy, remain focused; there will be a day when the world will stand up for you. What I dreamed and couldn't achieve, you dream and achieve. Until then, you may remain human but with a divine spirit. What I mean by this is for you to follow your dreams and your decisions, whatever they may be. Your life is yours to make. But make sure to enjoy it too and share whatever you feel with others. You are not alone. Some say that bonds weaken a person, but I believe in our family; it is our bonds that serve as our greatest strength. Remember this.

I love you, and I wish you the best on your upcoming "trial"

*(I'm sure you know what I mean ☺). Until you're ready to talk
about it with me, I'll be waiting. The same goes for Mom. No
matter what happens, control the outcome. It's always been in
your hands.*

Take care, my dear son.

He was right. For months, I had been hiding this from my parents.
Dad's open reply relieved me of the pressure to do so. I wanted to
wait for the right time—when I was ready to let them know of what
happened. He was a smart man, and I couldn't stop smiling when
he wished me luck in my adventurous love life. The fact that he
wanted me to live life on my own terms gave me a sense of freedom
and confidence. His advice for controlling the outcome also had a
deeper meaning. Even if I were to fail in my love for Rose, I could
take the result and mold it in my own way. It would depend on how I
dealt with it. Failure was only a choice of perspective. I was thankful
for Dad's counsel. He certainly had his methods, and his wisdom
astounded me. It was one instance when I understood how lucky I
was to have him as my father. I thanked him in my reply:

Hi, Dad,

*Simply put, I would just like to thank you. I love you. I know
that I may have done wrong in not sharing this with you and
Mom, but I'm glad that you understand this and are willing to
let me bring it up when I'm ready. I'm in love with someone,
and it is an emotional entanglement. Though I have had several
friends during my time here in Sudan, I have very few to whom
I could relate well. Rose is one among my friends who shares
my ideals and views. Over the year, we've sort of become close
to each other.*

*I will be leaving in a week or so, setting off on the greatest
journey in my life. Although I persistently express my confidence
in handling the heat alone, I can't deny feeling miserable about*

leaving you, Mom, and Annie behind. Mom began grumbling about this a month earlier. While you and Annie aren't at home, I've spent most of my time in her company, trying to cheer her up. I want to be strong and show both of you that I can handle my own challenges—be it in life or in love. I wanted to do things on my own terms. I'm happy to know that you appreciate this.

Thanks so much for the advice. Especially the well wishes on my "trial." I understand and have taken to heart what you've said in your e-mail. I promise I will remember your words. I see this as a golden opportunity for us to really sit and talk to each other. Although I'm to leave in a few days, these small memories, no matter how ordinary they are, can last a lifetime. It's been a while since we had our routine conversations at night on the balcony. Maybe, if you want, we can have one more before I'm to leave. I would like that. You can smoke if you want as an added bonus!

I know that the outcome has always been in my hands, and I will do my best. I have never forgotten the sacrifices you have made for this family. I have never been able to share what I feel for this family openly, and it hurts me to know that I have very little time now to do so. But, at least, I'm happy that I came to this realization earlier. There are no special moments; I suppose it's up to us to make them special. So I have no qualms in saying that, starting today, I will do all that I can to live my life well, love my family, and—most importantly—make you and Mom proud.

For now, these words are the only things that I can offer to you. But do know this, my love for you, Mom, and Annie is endless. I've always admired you and want to emulate you in life. I'm going to Canada not only to study—but with a goal in my heart to prove that I can lead my own life and also support the family one day. You have given so much for me, and I want to start now by giving everything that I have for you.

There is a difference in knowing something and experiencing it. I believe experience is the highest benefactor one can have in life and that is why I chose to go to Canada, despite knowing that I would be far away from my family. The distance will be a trial of its own sort, and I will put it to good use. All I want to do is to see you and Mom happy. I will not disappoint you. The reason? I'm your son. You may not expect anything from me, but that is your opinion. As your son, I will do my best to make you proud. I will consequentially be motivated in life because of my goals for the sake of our family and my future. I love you, Dad. Thank you. Come home soon this evening. Mom's cooked up a feast!

CHAPTER 14

THE TIMES ARE CHANGING

"Life is perplexing. Within a moment's notice, you realize you are treading the memories of your past while looking toward the future. People come and go. Is this what life is all about? Separations and new beginnings? Life is indeed beautiful."

Dad and I got our chance to hang out on the balcony that night. It felt great to chat with him on these terms, and I was happy to see that he was having fun as well. Apart from my family, Sudan also seemed intent on making life difficult for me during my last days. It is a desert country, but it had been raining every day for a week. The weather had to be so beautiful just before my departure.

Mom used this situation to her advantage, teasing me that Sudan was "crying" for my departure. She had been silent for a few days, and I knew that reality was bearing down on all of us. She would give anything for me to stay behind, but she also wished the best for my future. I understood her inner struggles and tried to help her feel better.

The city and its community had become large parts of my life. I could recall all the wonderful moments and experiences I had during our four years in the country. I often paced around the balcony in the early hours of the day. I was going to miss the beautiful morning skylines, the colorful horizons, and the warm winds. During the week, we were also welcomed by a thunderstorm. It was quite a show of lightning and thunder. Dad, Mom, Annie, and I were setting up for a picnic out on the balcony, but we retreated to our apartment when lightning began flashing over our heads.

Dad kept quiet about my e-mail. I appreciated his support and the fact that he respected my privacy. Mom caught a glimpse of the poems I had written for Rose. She was suspicious when she found them on my desk and inquired about their purpose. I was clever enough to satisfy her suspicions with my answer.

September 4 was judgment day. I was expecting to leave Khartoum on September 10. This was my last opportunity to pay a visit to KAS before my final preparations. I had processed every scenario in my mind, but life had a surprise hidden up its sleeve. I had hoped to speak with Rose directly about my feelings and then give her the gifts. I had intended to do so in the school garden.

I met up with her after school, letting my driver know that I would take awhile to return. I had informed Annie of my agenda, and she wished me the best. I rushed off in search for Rose. I was beaming with hope and elation. A private conversation would give us space to share things with each other. When I noted the empty garden, my excitement rose to a fever pitch. I saw her at the library, but my excitement was cut short when I heard that she had a family emergency to tend to. I couldn't believe it. I had spent countless days envisioning the moment when I could tell her how I felt, but we could only have a short conversation.

"Hey! Great to see you! Is that the letter? Awesome. I've got to go now. I'm sorry I can't stay longer, but it's an emergency."

"Oh? Um, okay. Well, yeah, here's the letter. Read it when you feel like it, okay? No pressure. And I also wanted to give you some mementos. Hopefully you won't forget me." I was trying to come up with a better thing to say, but it wasn't working out.

"Forget you? No way! Thanks so much! I wish we could talk a little longer, but take care and give me a call before you leave. When's your flight anyways?"

I could see that she was in a hurry. I hated this. "It's on September

10. I will be here in Khartoum, but I won't get a chance to see you again. Little busy with final preparations, so yeah, I suppose it is good-bye for now. Let me know what you think of the letter, okay?"

"Yep! For sure! Give me a call before you leave, okay? Anyways, I've really got to rush now. Take care. I'm going to miss you! Toodles!" She gave me a quick hug and rushed out of the library.

For a few minutes, I stood still, wondering what had happened. Everything I had planned, it had gone, well, like shit. This was supposed to be the day, but I had never gotten the chance to tell her how I felt. When she had hugged me, I wanted to hold her and whisper in her ear, in that brief space of time, those three words. Reality had taken the upper hand on this occasion. All my efforts for days—and it ended like this? Give me a break!

I felt frustrated and had a large desire to punch something or someone. I met Tina in the parking lot where she was awaiting her ride. Giving her a few mementos, I provided a short summary of what had happened. Her car pulled up just as I finished the story.

Tina said, "Man! That sucks, bro! Damn. You couldn't tell her? But at least look at it this way—you gave her the letter. I'm sure she'll respond soon. Don't worry about it. Also, you better call me before you leave. I can see you are bummed out, but cheer up; the exciting stuff is yet to begin. My driver doesn't like it when I keep him waiting, so I'm going to take off. Keep up hope—and let me know how things pan out for you and Rose. Thanks for the memento. I am going to miss you, but we will keep in touch, all right? Anyways, I love you. Take care. Bye!"

Tina's reply was somewhat comforting. I waved good-bye to my dear friend. She was right about everything. I knew I should have taken my chances earlier. I suppose I had to make do with what had happened. I had given the letter to Rose—now I had to wait for an answer.

Annie accompanied me as I walked around school for the rest of the evening, bidding farewell to Rino and the teachers. Our last stop was by the garden. I told Annie to tell the driver to be ready. She understood my need for privacy and set off immediately. I stood for a while underneath the tree, looking around the garden, absorbing every detail of my environment. I found it hard to believe that I was at this venture.

The school had served as a secondary home for four years. The garden was a precious place for me; it had accommodated me in my struggles and at my best. I knew I would cherish the memories I had in the garden for a long time to come. A sudden gust of wind brought me back to reality, and I felt a rush of leaves sweep into the air. Everything about the garden reminded me of my past.

It felt as if I was at a turning point. Behind me stood the wonderful memories with my family and friends, supporting and reminding me of where I came from. Ahead of me was the future—with bright expectations and promises. I smiled upon this realization, knowing I still had a long way to go. I was happy that I had the chance to return to Sudan, and I felt it was perfect to leave things this way. I turned around to make my way to the parking lot when a slight breeze dropped a leaf on my shoulder. It felt as if the garden was wishing me farewell too.

I observed the faint tints of yellow among the green patterns of the leaf. Autumn was approaching. It had been a wonderful summer. Smiling once again, I blew the leaf into the air and continued to the parking lot. My memories at KAS were finally over, and I was happy that it had ended this way.

I was going to miss this place. As we rode in the car, I silently thanked KAS for all that it had given me. My memories would serve me well for the future. As the school vanished in the distance, I smiled gently, and patting my heart, as if in comfort, said, "I promise to return one day. Thank you for everything."

* * *

After my last visit to KAS, I was busy for the remaining week. Thanks to Tina and Annie, I got frequent updates from school. I was too nervous to ask Rose if she had read the letter, but she was persistent in maintaining silence. Tina informed me later that Rose had loved the gifts, but she hadn't read the letter yet. I wondered why Rose hadn't said that to me directly.

It was possible that I would be out of the country before I heard what Rose had to say about my letter. It would make things difficult, but I had to live with it. With the help of Mom and Dad, I was able to pack up everything I needed. I also had some entertaining discussions with Dad. He advised me about university life and warned me not to get distracted by emotional entanglements. On the lighter side, he also encouraged me to enjoy life as much as possible and inform him immediately if I found a suitable woman for him in Canada. This remark resulted in a handful of slaps on the shoulder from Mom.

By September 7, everything was set. My visa was to arrive the following day, and my flight was confirmed for September 10. I decided to enjoy the last three days as much as possible with my family. I still hadn't heard any updates from Rose, but it didn't seem to matter. I didn't mind if she took her time. I would be happy to know if she reciprocated my feelings. Leaving for Canada would separate us for a while, but I knew we could brave the distance. At the same time, I was preparing for disappointment. No matter what happened, I would never forget that summer. It would be an arduous journey to move on if my love was one-sided, but I didn't want to worry about it. All I wanted to do was enjoy the last few moments with my family.

I spent my nights planning my return to Sudan in a year. I accumulated a bunch of pictures of my family and friends for the journey. They would keep me company during my time in Canada. I was going to miss them all so much. I felt sad and excited about leaving. I wouldn't be surprised if I cried on the day of my departure.

* * *

My final day in Sudan was blissful. I finally realized how much I would miss Mom, Dad, and Annie. I understood the value of family and the strengths of our relationships. I had made a promise to myself that I wouldn't cry, but my heart fluttered whenever I interacted with my family.

When we lived in India, it was customary to sleep on the floor on mats or sheets. When Annie was a baby, Mom, Dad, and I slept in her company in the main hall at our house. This prompted late-night chats on several occasions. Mom would fall asleep, and Dad would recite stories for Annie and me. Remembering those days made me wish I could be a kid again. On my last night in Sudan, we decided to do the same thing.

Mom and Dad's master bedroom was the preferred location. There wasn't enough space for all of us on the bed, so Dad and I did some weight lifting and carried the mattress from my room and made another bed. We had a huge gambling rally that night. Annie took the role of photographer throughout the game and flashed the camera at every opportunity. I was having great fun; being with them made all the difference. We drowned ourselves in each other's happiness. It was the best we could do to confront the reality that we would be in separate corners of the world the following day. Going to sleep that night was tough.

I was anxious about my journey. I would miss everything about Sudan. In four years, I had come to recognize Khartoum as my home—even more than India. Mom and Annie went to sleep after we finished gambling around midnight. I took a break and went out to the balcony to have a final look at Sudan's night sky.

As I stepped out the door, I was bathed in moonlight. The moon was at its gibbous phase; despite the brightness of the sky, I saw a cluster of stars. I had spent countless days pacing the balcony, observing the stars, and identifying constellations. I was easily able to identify Orion. The stars seemed to stay the same, yet several years had passed for me. So many things had changed, and I was looking forward to a new adventure.

At one point, I heard the window creak open and saw Dad looking for me. I remained quiet and waited to hear if he had anything to say, but the window closed again. I believe he knew that I wanted this moment alone, and I appreciated his gesture. Gazing up at the night sky, I felt a great sadness in my heart. After a while, I realized I had stood in the same spot for at least an hour. Time's flow was invisible on such occasions. Eventually, I made my way back to the bedroom. Annie was fast asleep in bed with Mom. Dad and I shared the extra mattress. It took me awhile to fall asleep, but soon enough, I lost myself to my dreams.

I woke up quite late the next morning. It took a lot of poking, hugging, and yanking from Annie to get me to my feet. Time passed faster than I wanted it to. Everything on that day had been arranged for me. We watched a wonderful Tamil family movie during lunch. Mom and Dad encouraged me to sleep after lunch, but it was a failed attempt. Instead, we spent the time talking about possibilities and goals for the following year. It was an emotional talk; Mom held my hands through it all. Our feelings for each other were overwhelming.

Before I left for the airport, several of Dad's colleagues came along to bid farewell. I managed to send Rose and Tina a few text messages between all of this. We had a series of last-minute family pictures before we set off for the airport. I took a last look at my home, visiting every single room, niche, and corner. I didn't want to miss a single detail. It was a small apartment, but it held four years of memories. The moment was bittersweet.

It was like a movie reel. We made a slow procession to the car. Each and every step took me away from home. I wanted to take things slowly. The airport was only a few minutes away from our apartment, but there was heavy traffic. I rolled down the windows and felt a hot breeze brush my face. The delicate, sandy smell of the air and the night sky—everything I saw had a memory attached to it. I struggled to hold back my tears. Mom held my hand throughout the ride. Everybody remained silent.

I reminded myself to call Tina and Rose before I boarded the plane. Once we reached the airport, I bid farewell to Mom and Annie near the entrance to the terminal. Dad had an official pass, allowing him through the security checkpoints that were restricted only to passengers. Mom was crying, but Annie remained stoic. Dad went off to clear my luggage. I didn't know what to say, but I held Mom and Annie in a deep hug, hoping that my actions could comfort them at this moment when words were useless.

I was excited to set off to my future, but I felt sad about leaving my family. All I could do was remain strong so I could give them confidence and hope that everything would be fine and that I would be back in their arms very soon.

Leaving Mom and Annie by the entrance, I joined Dad, and we passed through the security checkpoints. Dad hooked me up on his cell phone; while he completed my documents for the flight, I spoke with Mom and Annie. Mom's crying was relentless. It crushed my heart to hear her sobbing on the other side of the phone. They had been escorted to a balcony overlooking the departure terminal. Although I knew they were looking my way, I faced the opposite direction to avoid their tearful visages. It was to keep myself from breaking down.

Mom eventually passed the phone to Annie. Her voice choked as she tried to brush her tears away. I was going to miss her so much. I loved her beyond anything in the world. "Annie, I want you to know I will always love you. No matter the distance, I'm always there for you, okay? If you have any problem, don't hesitate to send me an e-mail or a note. I'm always here for you. Don't cry for me. I need you to be strong for Mom and Dad. Be there for them in my place. I love you so much."

"Sorry. Okay. I will stop crying. I'm going to miss you so much. Why do you have to go? Yeah, I get it's for university, but screw you for leaving me behind. I hate this. I want to hate you for leaving us behind, but I can't stop loving you at the same time. I love you so much, bro. I will miss you. Take care of your health." Annie's sobs were evident throughout the conversation.

"I will, sis. Don't worry about me."

"Oh yeah. Do you have anything to tell to Rose or Tina? I know you haven't received any news about the letter, but do you have anything to say before you leave?"

"I plan to give them both a call before I board, but in case I don't catch them, pass this message. For Tina, let her know that I wish her the best for her final year at KAS and that she should keep in touch. I'm grateful for all her help and will miss her sorely. For Rose, let her know that I was sorry to bring it up at the wrong time, and that I am waiting for her answer. Now pass the phone to Mom."

Mom had cried her tears away, but her voice was hoarse. "My son—"

"Mom, let me speak for a few minutes. I just want to let you know that I love you. I know this will be difficult for all of us. I aim to finish up as soon as possible and return home. Take care of yourself and Dad. I'm going to miss you so much. I love you."

"I know that you do, my son. I love you too. Take care of your health—and give us a call once you arrive in Canada safely. Love you, my son, and I wish you the best for your future. I'll be awaiting your return."

After these departing words, I accompanied Dad to the departure lounge. I waved vigorously at Mom and Annie as we moved into the boarding terminal, and they vanished from my sight. My flight was at midnight. Dad stayed with me for an extra hour before he left. Though I just wanted to have a few personal words with him, we couldn't help talking about official plans for university. Time was flying by.

Dad gave me a final hug, smiled with pride, and said, "You'll be fine. Be strong and do well. Your family is always there for you. I'm always here for you. Remember that, okay?"

"Yes, Dad. I will do my best." I knelt down on the floor to receive his blessings. Following a strong pat on the back and a confident smile, Dad walked away. Nearing the exit, he turned around and gave me a final wave before he disappeared. I remained stationary for a while, staring at the spot where he had vanished, before sitting down and clutching my heart. All of a sudden, I felt completely alone.

Dad's words kept me strong; within a few minutes, I felt better. It was imperative that I remained confident. The promises I had made to Dad awakened the fire in me. I had a purpose and responsibility in Canada, and I would make Mom and Dad proud.

Tina called me a few minutes later. Annie had informed her of my departure and had passed along my message. Tina was enthusiastic throughout the conversation; she wished me well for the future and asked me to keep in touch. We recalled our first meeting and laughed at the circumstances of our friendship. By the end of our conversation, we were both looking forward to a reunion in the near future. We bid farewell without regret.

I felt optimistic about the future after talking to Tina, but I hadn't received a call from Rose. I took it upon myself to give her one. There was only half an hour left before I was to board the flight. I was disappointed to hear a message that her phone was either turned off or busy. Not willing to give up, I kept texting and calling until I boarded the flight.

I flew from Khartoum to Jeddah, with a stop in Frankfurt, Germany; my final destination was Edmonton. Once I boarded the plane and settled down, I was prompted to turn off my phone. I felt a twinge of regret and disappointment at not having heard from Rose. I spent a few seconds deciding what to say to her in one final text message. I wrote, "I'm missing you already. Good-bye, Rosie, and take care."

From the window, I could see my apartment building on the far side of the runway. This was going to be a long journey, and I would have to endure it alone. As the plane prepped for takeoff, I reached into my wallet and pulled out my photos. There were a bunch of pictures with Mom, Dad, and Annie from the night before as well as a few with Rose and Tina at Rider's Diner. I also had a picture of my friends and teachers at KAS. Just about everyone was with me.

As the plane took off, my heart was laden with grief, but I was comforted by a beautiful sight that held me once we flew through the clouds. It was the full moon. It lay by the horizon of a vast surface of clouds blanketing the sky and separating me from the earth. I remembered when my family had taken a trip to Kodaikanal. During our drive along the mountain, we had encountered a thick fog. We didn't know what was on the other side, but when we made it through, we had a beautiful view of the hill station on the mountainside. I had been inspired to write a poem about the experience.

I didn't know what the future held, but with the support of my family, friends, and loved ones, I knew I could pull through. Like the time in Kodaikanal, my poem's title perfectly described this experience: "A Mist of Heaven."

I spent the trip in solitude, thinking about my four years at Sudan. Through all the ups and downs, everything had turned out fine. Looking at the photos, I realized the wealth of memories I had. I conversed silently with the people in the photos until I fell asleep.

I dreamed of my return home and being with my family. I also dreamed of my first meeting with Rose and our good times at KAS. When I woke up, my grief had been replaced by feelings of love, responsibility, faith, and joy. It was just the beginning of a long journey, but I wouldn't give up easily.

Upon arrival in Canada, as I took my first step off the plane and looked around, I felt strong. I would miss my parents, friends, KAS, and Sudan, but I had to move on. I had to follow my future. The times were changing, but I felt strongly that—no matter what happened—if I was willing to keep heart, all would be well.

I was eager to finish my first year at university and return to Sudan. I felt content in the knowledge that I would see my family and friends in the near future. I felt their presence supporting me wherever I went. All I had to do was remember and cherish the memories of the past, live the present, and anticipate the future.

A new day had come, and life was where I was going.

A NEW BEGINNING

"From the day I was born till the day I die, I intend to believe that life will always provide an answer. In fact, I'll take my chances with that."

Two to three years have passed since my last visit to Sudan in the summer of 2010. After my first year of studies at the University of Alberta, I returned home to visit my family and friends. During this period of time, which I now call our last summer, I came to terms with the end and a new beginning to the odyssey of love, family, and friendship that I discovered during the span of my life in Khartoum.

After departing to continue my second year of studies, my family moved to Sierra Leone when my dad's contract in PLAN Sudan ended in September 2010. I am in the final year of my undergraduate degree, writing the last few pages of my amazing journey.

Upon leaving Sudan on September 10, 2009, to pursue my higher studies, my return in 2010, and the continuation of my studies from September 2010 to 2013, I confronted several challenges. I grew up like any other young man.

My trials originated from the legacy I left behind at KAS from 2009 to 2010. I wrestled with my memories of what had occurred in our last summer as well as adapting to my new life in Edmonton. From 2011 to 2012, I gradually accepted the circumstances of my past, maturing beyond the shell of a teenager, into a young man who is confident and enjoying his new life.

On particular occasions, I look back happily to the wonderful memories of my life in Sudan. Although several years have passed, it still feels as if it was yesterday when I was enrolling at KAS and meeting my friends. Now, we are all spread around the world. Our bonds are kept together by our memories from KAS, but we have learned to follow our futures happily.

My time in Edmonton has helped me understand several things. It was sort of like a proving ground. In my isolation, I learned to take responsibility for my life. I learned the importance of family, love, and friendship. Most of all, I learned to live life without regrets and to pursue my dreams diligently. I've realized, after all these years, that as long as one has the heart to persevere, life has a way of letting you know that things will always work out in the end.

It would take more than words to explain all the gifts life has granted me in these few years. I would like to look back to when this exodus began with my arrival in Canada.

* * *

Parting is such sweet sorrow. That is how it felt to be away from my family and friends. Living on the other side of the world was an experience with its share of happiness, sorrow, and new meanings.

Due to the delay in my visa, I arrived two weeks late for university. I initially found it difficult to catch up with my studies, especially in my honors courses. The sinking feeling of isolation and distance afflicted me every time I returned to my dormitory. Within a few days of my arrival, I made friends. Over time, I was well known among my floor's community and by my peers. It was a new environment, and I learned a new reality.

It felt weird to live my own life. I played by my own rules. I still depended on my parents' financial support, but I was alone in Edmonton and had to balance my studies and social life without the counsel of my family. I spent the first two weeks adapting to my new environment. I put pictures of my family on the walls of my room.

I listened to music I had always loved, and I dreamed of Sudan. In one way, it kept me up and about.

Dad told me that distance provides perspective toward the value of someone or something you've always cherished. I felt the sweet pain of separation from my family and friends. Dad eventually joined me for two weeks in Edmonton. He had a conference in Toronto and decided to use the opportunity to visit me. His presence made me feel at home, and his counsel gave me spirit and strength to continue facing and overcoming my challenges at university.

Dad stayed with me for a week. We had several chats about my expectations for the future. In the evenings, we took walks around the city—oblivious to the cold—talking and laughing together. Dad mentioned that he was proud to see me studying abroad and handling my life independently. Hearing about Annie, Mom, and the desolate state of our apartment since my departure broke my heart. My family was struggling to come to terms with my absence.

Dad regretted that time had flown so fast and that he had never had the chance to see his son grow up. He shared his pride, delight, and joy to see where I was. He felt it made up for what he had missed during my childhood. I didn't blame him at all; I was just glad to have him there with me.

After his conference in Toronto, Dad departed from Canada. I kept in touch with my family through frequent talks on Skype. With the added strength, clarity, and support that Dad had given me, I regained my vigor toward my studies and pushed forward with my new life in Edmonton.

I realized it was shameful to focus on my isolated status. It was time to keep my promise to make Mom and Dad proud. Consequently, I began to take responsibility for my life. My routine was simple: study, make friends, have a good time, enjoy life, finish the year, and return home.

Time is relative. Given this mind-set, I was able to enjoy my days at university. Once in a while, I did some soul-searching and withdrew to my thoughts. I took walks, gazed at the night sky, or conversed with my inner voice. Such leisurely activities helped me organize my thoughts and find answers to my questions. I learned that life wasn't meant to be discovered—it was created uniquely by individual choices.

I received several e-mails and letters from my family during my time in Edmonton. Their words were always a source of comfort. Several of these letters spanned pages, particularly when I was trying to settle in.

My dearest son,

I was quite excited when I saw your e-mail. Good to know that everything went well for you. Your father and I saw your airplane from the terrace, and it was really an emotional moment. We are thinking of you all the time.

Until now, there is no news for dad from the Canadian Embassy. Keep note of things that you want him to bring.

All the best, my son, and I wish you good luck in all your endeavors. Have a wonderful time at university.

God bless you.

Your one and only Mom

Beloved son,

So thrilled to see your letter and to know about your happiness and challenges.

My first advice: take it easy. You can do anything. Don't worry about the complexity of the lessons. Relax. This is just the beginning. I don't advise you to exert all your steam. Take it cool.

Once you are cool, you can reflect and see your strength and stamina to cope up with your selections (subjects). Whatever you feel is best for you, you are the one to decide. You can always consult your professors. As far as I have noted from you, whatever you have felt difficult in the beginning, you have done very well later.

I was laughing when you said how you missed your classes (locations). You will become familiar with the area soon. Understand that you missed all the initial inductions. So don't be hard on yourself.

I don't expect you to write so much, as I understand you must be so busy in settling down. Take it easy. You can write later when you get free.

Please do not isolate yourself. Mingle with your classmates; get to know your professors and people around. The only thing you have to be careful of is not to be influenced by peer pressure. You can politely refuse in such situations. They are not wrong. It is a culture there. You have to learn to be in there and out of it at the same time.

Never feel you are alone. You are here with us all the time, and we are with you.

Recite a rosary every day, my son. Mother Mary will intercede for you with Jesus, and you will be fine.

Enjoy your new life with confidence and positive attitude.

The best steel must go through fire. This is what Sr. Rosary (my mentor) told me when I was at your age.

With hugs and kisses,

Dad

* * *

I decided not to purchase a cell phone due to the expense. I could account for such a purchase once I acquired a part-time job; until then, my communication with friends and family was restricted to e-mail or Skype. It was good enough for my family and me. Our conversations on Skype would continue for several hours. In one conversation, I related my entire history with Rose to Mom and Dad.

Dad feigned the act of being unaware of my love affair with Rose—though he received quite a scolding from Mom once I let her in on the story. Mom's reaction was surprisingly positive, but she maintained a stern attitude as she advised me to make sure that my social life didn't disrupt my academic focus. She was pretty quick to pick up on the hints I had dropped regarding this issue during the summer. She said, "It is up to you to decide what you have and what you want to have in life. Remember, we don't go discovering our rights and wrongs—it just happens. Love is somewhat similar and is an essential quality of life. Your life is in your hands. But know this—you are at a fragile stage of your maturity. In these moments, the smart man wouldn't make any big decisions. I tell this to you, but I leave it up to your choice if you approve my counsel. I'm proud of you, and I always will be because I know that you will make the right decisions. Thanks for sharing this with me, son, and don't hesitate to do so for anything else in the future."

University continued, and my social life in Edmonton was thriving. I faced new challenges and met various people with different personalities. It felt like a grand adventure. My field of study was astrophysics; consequently, I was the butt of many jokes. Many of my friends teased me about how useless my field of study would be in the future.

At times I felt angry, but I maintained my composure. I realized that, unlike me, several others were still indecisive about what careers they wanted to pursue. I'd had the dream of being an astronomer since childhood, and I was happy enough to know that my path was set. I refrained from judging my friends, but I found great happiness in helping others. As such, I gained recognition among my peers.

My actions taught me to understand different perspectives and confront the varying viewpoints of my friends and peers. Such experiences also opened me up to newer venues in life where my personal ideals, beliefs, and judgment were put to test. I sensed that I was changing into a different person.

I began developing new philosophies in life. Mom and Dad had always said that the twenties was the age of romance. For me, love became my life. I enjoyed my life, loving what I had for myself, and I helped others love life's beauty. It felt great. Rather than asking for things I wished in prayer, I supplicated and thanked God for the things I had. In this manner, I found great friends who touched my life in ways I could never have imagined. As much as I shared my experiences with them, I also learned from theirs.

I found a new home in Edmonton. I also learned how difficult friendship is. Friendship felt like peeling an onion. It can hurt your eyes and bring tears to your cheeks, yet when all the peeling is done, you realize you are content—and there is still more left to it. Friendship was also a rainbow with various spectrums. Everyone I met had a different approach to life, and their personalities often left strong impressions on me.

My time in Edmonton began to manifest as a test of what I needed for myself and who I wanted to be. I wrote my daily experiences in my journal. Identity is a powerful concept. One's identity can be found in the company of a friend—or in sorrow, thoughts, or words. Through the words I wrote in my journal, I realized the truth about life: there was no truth—unless one wanted it to be.

This thought gave me the feeling of ultimate freedom. There were no truths to realize unless one maintained a sponsored truth. There were only truths to create. Through this, I fully understood what Dad had meant about life as more of a creation than a discovery. I relished in this epiphany. I felt as though I had finally created a small part of my own life, starting with this new interpretation. It was all an inspiration of my love for my family and friends.

Aside from my philosophical escapades, I still received daily messages from Tina and my other friends in Sudan. I was pleased to know that I hadn't become a memory to them. I missed Rose a lot and yearned to hear from her. Our memories together lingered in my mind day and night. I kept wondering about her possible answer. Eventually, I received an e-mail from Tina. She had talked with Rose about my letter. I learned from Tina that Rose had read the letter the day I had given it to her. She had expressed surprise at its content, but she had refrained from providing her answer until I left so she wouldn't make a rash decision that could hurt Annie, Tina, or me.

I was puzzled by Tina's story and felt that this was not going to end well for me. At the same time, I wanted to hear what Rose had to say. I sent her a few e-mails for an answer. Had I succeeded—or did our friendship overweigh my love for her?

I expected some resistance, but her answer was immediate. I had always told myself to expect nothing from what was to happen. Yet when I read her message, it cut me deep. In one way, it made me fall even more in love with her.

Hey,

Sorry that I wasn't able to reply, but I heard you were waiting for an answer. I understand that you want to share your feelings and not hide anything from me. My first reaction to your letter was just surprise, nothing else. You said that I might be angry or confused, right? Well, here's my thought on that: There was no reason for me to be angry. It's not a crime to love someone. I'm not confused since I already know how I feel. I simply felt surprised when I read the letter. In truth, I read it the day you gave it to me. I didn't tell you, Annie, or Tina until a little more than a month later. I didn't tell anyone because I didn't want to make a mistake that would hurt all of you. So I thought it over, and I admit, wrong timing.

I'm sure you want to know my answer right now. Yeah. I feel, for now, we should stay friends. To tell you the truth, your letter was too much. It became a bit burdensome to me.

It was a bit of pressure. You kept saying that it would be okay if I didn't feel the same way, but I know that there is no way to avoid any pain. Not just to you—but to your sister and me as well.

Annie really cares a lot for you. So it kills me that I'm in the position of writing this to you. This is not the first time I've said these words to someone, and it's really painful. People always think that the victim of love is always the one to suffer, but I think that the person who is to decide that victim's fate is also placed in an equally compromising position. I hope you understand that.

I don't have time to write more, but this is really difficult for me. I do hope you understand.

I'll talk to you later then.

Bye.

Though her letter hinted at indecision and my persistence for finding a solution, it left me with a difficult choice of holding on to what I felt for her or moving on with my life. The ambiguity of her words resulted in confusion, and I wished to speak to her directly. I felt the situation was similar to when I had waited for Rigel's answer.

I couldn't deny that I was disappointed, but another side of my heart struggled to keep hope. I couldn't accept the fact that it was over—or I was too greatly in love with her. I was tortured by my choices for months. I wanted to remain ignorant of these decisions, but I felt their nagging presence every time I was alone in my room, thinking about her.

She had described my letter as a burden. My love was a burden to her. I couldn't take that. Rose and I didn't keep in touch consistently for the next few months. Once in a while, I would send her an e-mail, but she wouldn't respond. I had mentioned that if my love failed, I still wanted to be her friend. Her letter had given me the impression that she was deeply hurt by what had happened. I couldn't know for sure how she felt, but her reluctance to respond didn't sit well with me.

I reread the letter I had written to her. I had poured my heart out and expressed my love for her. If I had been in her place, making a similar decision, I would have felt the same way. I had expressed my love strongly—and that had been my mistake. Although I had been open to being disappointed, I had not accounted for her feelings. The strength of my feelings was the cause of her burden and pain. I wondered if that was why she didn't respond to my e-mails. Was she seeking distance? Had I done wrong? Was my decision to salvage my love for her a turn for the worse? Had I hurt the person I loved the most by revealing my love for her?

These questions were accompanied by an unforgivable guilt. Despite my open-mindedness and expectations, I realized I may have jeopardized our friendship. I knew I had to do something, but I was helpless since I was thousands of miles away from her. Dad had advised me to control the outcome. But what could I do when the outcome itself was in question? I was still in love with her.

I struggled to make a decision. Once again, I fell into confusion and denial—denial of what had happened and confusion about what I should do. At university, I had often seen close friends of mine delve into relationships. When things didn't even out, they would break up and continue with their own lives. Whenever I talked to them about their past relationships, I sensed that they ignored or denied the existence of any feelings toward their partner—no matter how long the relationship had been. It was as if they were ignoring that part of their life and equating it to nonexistence.

I couldn't do that. I couldn't just ignore what I had felt for Rose. I couldn't just throw it away. If I had to, it would mean the end of our friendship. Despite knowing that she didn't feel the same way about me, I wanted to be her friend. If I couldn't love her, I had to fight for the right to love her as a friend. How could I achieve this without causing further pain or burdening our relationship? There had to be a solution.

Questions ran through my mind. As the days passed, I grew more anxious to return home. The day I could see her would be a joyous occasion. It would give me the chance to right my wrongs and renew our friendship—if possible. I sought the help of Tina and my close friends back home on what course of action I should follow. I knew that this decision was ultimately in my hands. I was lost.

I passed my first semester at university by exhausting my thoughts and feelings about this situation. It hit me that I had said "I love you" to Rose. I couldn't retract those words if I had to under this scenario. I wouldn't have because, deep in my heart, although distancing myself from such a thought, I knew I was still in love with her.

Mom, Dad, and Annie perceived my emotional turmoil. I appreciated their support and advice, but the decision was my responsibility. Nothing could change that. I had yet to control the outcome. I had informed Annie about these new developments once I received Rose's e-mail. I knew she was hurting too. She had always wanted to see us together. I wasn't surprised when she told me to move on and stop thinking about Rose. But I couldn't.

Whatever was to happen between us would have to wait until I returned so I could resolve my questions with her directly. I waited in anxiety for the year to end. I waited until I could find an answer. I didn't know what I was hoping for. I was still in love with Rose, wishing that time could bring us together. After all, she had said, "For now, let's just stay friends."

* * *

On December 5, I gave a poem to Dad for his birthday:

The Guide

He took my arm
And lifted me up.
With a tender kiss,

189

He opened my world.
On his shoulders,
I spent my time.
His laughter and happiness
Mingled with mine.
Unconscious I was
To these things
At those initial times,
But now I remember, and I cherish those memories as mine.
Years have passed in minutes,
And in the sudden departure to the future,
I now feel every minute away from his side,
Like a year.
You were always by my side,
And I will always be by yours.
One as a shadow of another,
Together we will be forever.
Father and son
Are two different words,
But father and son
Share one united world.
Though we remain far away,
Your guidance still shows me the way.
I hold your wisdom in my mind,
And I hold your love in my heart.
Days may pass
Until we meet,
But at this moment of happiness,
I find you sitting in the opposite seat.
Not a moment passes
Without you in my mind.
I will make you proud.
Don't you worry about it all.
The future may be anxious,

The past may be painful,
But we are now in the present,
And it is for us to realize it is beautiful.
You were always there by my side
When I was young,
When I needed you.
Now I want you to know that I'm by yours and always will be.
As your son,
I give you these words,
And I wish you
Happy Birthday, my dear father; you have always been my world.
In dedication to my dear father
Do I this poem write,
Letting him know,
Who has been my guide in life,
That I will always be in his sight,
Just as he will always be in mine.
Happy Birthday, Dad! I love you!

Dad enjoyed the poem and conveyed this to me via a long e-mail. By mid-December, I had completed my semester exams. Winter break set in. The residence was nearly abandoned since many students returned home for Christmas. I didn't mind the isolation. It gave me a sense of peace.

Busy with my own preparations for the following semester, and eagerly awaiting the arrival of Christmas, my mind deviated from any thoughts about Rose. It was my first Christmas away from my family. In that sense, I did feel lonely. After attending sermon on the eve of Christmas, I returned to my dorm. It was late, and I spent my time cooking in the common kitchen and listening to Christmas carols. While waiting on the curry and rice, I checked my e-mail. I had received two beautiful poems from Annie.

That Someone Is You

I've waited so long for someone like you
A person who knows me so well, who knows all truths
I hide nothing from you, you know all my secrets
You come to me when I shed tears
You're there for me when I need a friend
Our bond has grown as time had passed
And I found someone
That someone is you
I've always wanted a brother like you
The love you give shall always be pure
You share with me our memories of life
And there flows a river, a river that never stops
A river that goes forever more
And you know what the river holds?
It holds you and me together as one piece
And in that river, I found someone special
That someone is you
You always have and always will be part of my heart
I'll love you forever
And I wish that upon the road I travel from this day on
You'll not be ahead of me
Nor behind me
But beside me, holding my hand, ready to face what is to come
I know someone who has a pure heart
I know someone who loves with all his might
I know someone who knows what's right
I'm so lucky to have met someone like you
But I'm making a mistake
There is no one like you
You are special
You are unique
And you are more than just a someone

You are my brother
I love you
Dedicated to you, my amazing bro!

The Friend I Never Had

I woke up one day, feeling different
Feeling as if a part of me had been torn away
A true love I thought existed
Had been broken apart in a split second
Feeling like a person without a heart
I roamed around, wandering, having nowhere to go
But then you welcomed me with your smile
Your smile so bright that it made my day
Even a small thing you do makes me happy
You can make me fly when I'm down without uttering a single word
You are the beating of my heart
You are a huge part of my soul
The road we share together never ends
Its path goes forever more
And we take the same steps together
One step at a time
You don't need to come back
When you've gone
You're always inside me
In my heart
You are the world to me
And, hopefully, I'm yours too
To me, you are everything
You are the axis that spins the earth
The god that holds the sky
The heart that beats inside
You are the support I've always wanted
The love I've always needed

The smile that lights up my day
You are the friend I've never had
And I know you'll always be.

* * *

I was happy to hear from my family; the following day, we conversed for hours on Skype. Once in a while, Annie would annoy me by presenting the delicious sweets and foods Mom had prepared for Christmas. I missed being home, but I was grateful to have my family for company. It was a unique Christmas. I was happy and felt supported by the love for my family. The distance between us seemed like an illusion.

The next few weeks passed quickly. As second semester approached, my anxiety opened up like a sore wound. I consulted Dad about my personal struggles with Rose.

Dear son,

Thanks for sharing your anxiety with me. My first advice: relax. It is natural to come across these feelings and thoughts. When you relax, you will gain clarity. It is unfortunate that I'm not available to speak to you directly about this on Skype, but let me give you some reflections. Where is the question of such "self-searching" coming from? It can happen when you are depressed or when you are in love.

Are you depressed? Say, for discussion, that you are. About what? I know that you currently miss your family and friends. But I believe that someday or another you have to be on your own. Due to my family's financial status, I was brought up in an orphanage, alone. I had no one to care for me. But you are not like that. You have us. Of course we are far away. But Mom and Annie are always in touch with you.

You are there in Canada on a mission that came from your own interest for astrophysics. It is not an easy subject for normal people. I believe you are a wonder kid, and someday you will show your genius to the world. Remember, all geniuses are eccentrics. They experience such questions and thoughts. It is their passion that becomes the driving force in shaping their destiny. As long as you are passionate, nothing can distract you. You will certainly not feel lonely or depressed. It is similar to the mission that takes the determination of a soldier in war.

It is also possible that you are feeling this way because you are in love. When you are in love, you sometimes feel lonely, especially when you are away from that person. It is natural. At this moment, when you are away from family and friends, when such experiences occur, you will find yourself a bit confused. All I can tell you is to take your time. As long as your love inspires you to do greater things, it is true love. Love should not divert you from your path.

Now, on to the next reflection: you mentioned that you are able to guide others with their lives. As a friend, you can comfort others, counsel, and help. But you don't decide for them. Everybody's life is their own. There may be several reasons for your anxiety. But I know that you can persevere and make it through. Family, love, friendship, culture, religion, and environment can all be influences.

You should try to find your own inner balance. I will support you and guide you, but at the end of the day, you must find it for yourself. I have always admired your maturity in dealing with such issues. But I've also noted your weakness. You are quick to get emotionally entangled. If you think about it, you will see how quickly you are affected by the issues that surround you. Am I right? I can't be wrong. Why? Because you are me.

I was just like you at your age, but for many years. It was very difficult to come out of this habit—even though I realized all those people that I loved in life, that I cared and gave so much for, walked on their own ways without looking at me.

I've never been ungrateful or hurtful to others, but I learned that at the end of the day, everyone walks their own path. I have become a stronger person, and that's the same I wish to see of you. When you listen to others, listen with your heart, but when you reflect, reflect with your mind. It is your life—and your life alone. Nobody is going to make your decisions except you.

Mom, Annie, and I will always support you in whatever makes you happy. Having said that, all I'm telling you to do is to relax and see the "real reason" that makes you feel this way. I'm proud of you. I know you will find your way. Let not the passing clouds trouble you. The sky is clearer if you calmly look at it with your eyes wide open. You have then started your journey. There will always be ups and downs. Otherwise, life wouldn't be exciting. But at the same time, when you keep thinking and dreaming about your destination, your journey and resolve will get stronger.

Enjoy your time and relax.

With much love,

Dad

* * *

I followed Dad's advice. I knew the root of my uncertainties was my anxiety about Rose. I wouldn't have an answer until I returned to Sudan. It was understandable to be anxious, but it didn't do me any good if that anxiety was influencing my studies or other aspects of my life. I patiently waited for the end of the term, but I still faced my share of challenges. Mixed messages from friends at home often renewed my anxiety.

A letter from Tina nearly threw me off my track:

Bro! I've got some good news! You should thank me for being your awesome sister! Start sending Rose a lot of e-mails—even if she doesn't respond. I've been getting a lot of good vibes lately from her, and I think deep inside she really does like you. She's been talking about you all the time, ever since this winter break. It's always about how much she misses you.

With regard to the e-mails, I don't want you to send her love letters. Just be cool and act normal and talk about leisurely stuff like you did when you were with her at KAS. Just share stuff about your life over at university. You don't want to pressure her. But seriously, I'm so freaking happy for you! I'm jumping around in joy! You have no freaking idea, man!

I'm very sure that she likes you—and that's for who you are! I'm partying this weekend on behalf of your success. I just wanted to let you know! I know you are going to be very happy to hear this!

Take care, bro! I can't wait for your return (neither can Rose ☺ hahaha!).

Within a few seconds, my heartbeat was erratic. The overwhelming sense of satisfaction and happiness made me shout in joy for the next five minutes. I began punching the wall in excitement—until my neighbor punched his side. At that point, I resorted to punching my pillows instead. I wished I was in an open field where I could scream my lungs out in happiness. If this was true—wow!

I wrote a hasty reply:

Tina! I love you, sis! Thank you for such great news! You have made my day! Though I'm not completely sure that just because she is talking about me justifies her liking me, I'll take what you say, as it makes me really happy. I'll send her an e-mail, like you instructed. I've also passed the message on to Annie on Facebook. She will be very happy to hear about this.

Don't use this occasion to party! Go do your homework! Not! Party as much as you want! I'm going to be partying too! Drinks are on me! Though I don't drink, and you're not even here!

I'm freaking insane with happiness! I literally screamed

*when I read your e-mail and am jumping in joy! I can't wait
to return to Sudan to see the entire scenario unfold!*
  Thanks for being here for me, Tina! I love you! Take care!

I was tremendously happy to receive this news. Maybe there was
hope—some chance I could succeed. When the adrenaline dropped,
I was struck with more questions. Why did this have to happen now?
Why now—of all times? Months had passed since Rose's letter, and
our communication had been sparse. How was it possible that Rose
could even feel this way when she had mentioned that this feeling
was the cause of her burdens? It didn't seem to fit the overall picture.
Once again, reality dawned on me. I needed to hear this directly
from her. As before, mixed messages from my friends—or anyone
else—didn't help.

I kept my feelings in check, intending to justify them after I
returned to Sudan. I was still confused, but my decision to do so
gave me a sense of direction. It was particularly difficult when I felt
lonely or spent time writing poems about Rose and inadvertently
recalled memories of Sudan.

A Thousand Miles

Walking by your side,
We make our way through the crowd.
From the present,
I dream of our future.
But no matter what,
There always seems to be a thousand miles that set us apart.
You remain oblivious to my love,
But I'm willing to go all the way to prove it to you.
A thousand miles,
There may be between us.
But in my love,
I'm willing to cross it all just for you.

Sometimes I wonder
If I will ever make it through.
Following you wherever you go,
You're all I ever had.
The smile that you always give
Burns through my heart and makes me smile.
There is so much time,
Yet it passes me in a bliss.
You take my hand in yours,
So we can make the journey with each other.
But I wish you would take my heart in yours,
So we can live together forever.
I will be by your side
To keep you warm, to keep you protected, to give you my love.
I just want to love you forevermore
And hug you close like never before.
You will always be mine,
But I don't know what to do.
To get you to see me,
Will it take more than the life I see?
And I wonder,
Will there be a time we will be together again?
A little pain do I feel,
But in the hope of our love, I leave everything behind.
To keep on moving,
To be by your side at all times,
To let you know
I'm here waiting for you.
I'm here waiting for you
To see the love I have for you.
I'm here waiting for you
To hug and give me the kiss I had always wanted from before.
I remember feeling the warmth
Of the first hug that we had that one day.

That day, you supported me.
In your warmth, you dried my tears.
And that day,
My love for you awoke.
And now, even with these thousand miles,
I wish to sail away in love, with you by my side.
To give you the warmth
You once gave me.
To provide you the love
You awoke in me.
To make the thousand miles so long to be,
In our love, something very small indeed.

Standing in the Rain

I dreamed of that day every night,
But life has only made me wait.
So far away we were.
Not a moment passed when I haven't wished you were here.
Thoughts that I had for the future
Only led to our love's departure.
The more I tried to close my heart away,
The more the love I had for you made me sway.
I had always wished us to be together,
But, it seems, our love was not meant to be forever.
And without you by my side,
I felt I wanted to hide.
I know I have to confront the truth,
But my heart's broken to take the pain.
I wish to see you happy.
If this is fate, let it be this way.
Yet there remains one thing,
One thing I want to say.
Though we may now be apart,

I'll be here for you, as you always are in my heart.
I knew that you were someone special
When I first saw you that day.
But now, after all we've been through,
I never expected it would come to be this way.
I've lost my sense of time;
Yesterday becomes today.
All of a sudden, in this moment of separation,
I feel you are so far away.
It makes me wonder,
Was I just living a lie?
I just want to cry,
But there aren't any tears in my eyes.
It all makes me wonder again,
Was I just living a lie?
I'm lost in between decisions,
To hold on—or keep moving on.
I remember those words you said,
And I ask myself why.
Why did it have to be this way?
It has taken all this time.
Led by a false hope, I now feel betrayed.
Not by you or by our love,
But by life.
The future calls out to me,
But our past will always be.
I have no more to say;
Words will never be enough.
After having come here,
I realize it's time to say good-bye.
Time will pass,
But I will always remember this day.
I feel like I want to wait,
But I know our love can't stay.

There is yet one moment to come;
It is our last summer.
We have come to the crossroads,
And now it's time for us to part ways.
Writing what my heart feels,
Isolated and to my dismay,
I remember that day
Standing in the rain,
Waiting for you
To run to my side so I could take you in my arms.
I find myself again now
Standing in the rain.
Not waiting, but watching,
Both of us walking apart.
My heart breaks, and tears envelop my eyes,
But I'm not sure if it is the rain or if I am really crying.
But I know that you're one
I will never forget
'Cause it was also that day standing in the rain with you
I knew that I loved you
Written in the moment of departure
Of my love's truth.

Tears in the Dark

It has become so long
Since I wrote a love song,
For you, yearns my soul,
The one who makes me whole.
In your memories,
I comfort my sleep,
But in what the future holds,
I find my heart fall deep.
I reach for you

In my dreams,
The love that I had for you,
Still a passion I feel.
Melancholy,
Do I suffer?
Tears of a thousand hearts
That down my cheeks stream.
Without you
By my side,
I find myself afraid,
Turning toward the shadows to hide.
I seek your light
That made my life bright.
I still remember the day
When I held you in my arms, tight.
Life passes by
As never before,
But I'm unwilling to move along.
My heart is wanting more.
The road is difficult,
And I remain blind,
But in my persistent love for you,
I find the path again.
You remain, as you always did,
My hope, my power,
My pleasure,
My pain.
My life endures in the petals
Of our broken love.
Will it ever be the same again?
I don't know.
The morning star of my life,
I reach over for you again
As you sit down,

In the distant horizon.
And as darkness sets,
I close my eyes
And go to sleep again,
Wishing everything is a lie.
And in my dreams,
I find you again;
You are there,
Yet you are not really here.
Your smile cuts through my heart,
And I find myself falling,
In the wake of an abandoned love,
In the opening of a passionate experience.
How long can this be?
Nothing is what it seems,
And I am distraught.
In your arms, I want to remain.
But I finally open my eyes,
And I realize that it is not true.
It is all just a dream,
But I don't give up.
And in the end of it,
If I can only be with you in my dreams,
I'd rather sleep forever.

When I Saw You That Day

I sat in the corner,
Not knowing why,
Seeing nowhere,
Hearing nothing.
In my own world,
I remained in solitude.
Life seemed still,

Time not passing by.
But then, a faint rustle in the air,
A slight ripple in my heart,
A feeling that there was someone
Approaching.
I ignored,
But my heart gave way,
And I took the slightest turn to look
When life changed around me.
As I saw you
Approaching me around the same corner,
Which didn't seem familiar anymore,
Shouting out my name,
I could see, I could hear.
Love as pure as snow,
Every second seemed to pass faster,
And I stood up,
Your presence a new light in my world.
Never stop my heart.
And reaching out my arms,
I embraced you
As you hugged me back.
Love at first sight,
Love heartfelt,
Holding you tight,
I felt the world around me light.
Girl,
I knew you then.
I knew you were the right one for me
When I saw you that day.
Never stop my heart.
I live on within you,
Our love lives within us,
And together, in our love, our life lives on.

A moment in time
Of a feeling beyond anything else
Taking me even higher
Than I have ever felt in my life.
Like the bloom of the white rose in the winter,
Like the dewdrop in the first rain,
Like the light of the first dawn,
Like the birth of a true love.
Girl,
I fell in love with you
When I saw you that day.
By a feeling that had enveloped my heart for a few days,
I write this poem in the moment of a new pathway,
Looking toward the future.
I wait for your reply, Rose, my dear.

You're Everything

I miss you,
One place to hold
In my heart
Where I can feel you.
I want you.
You are the light
That guides me
In the dark.
I see you
In my dreams.
Reaching out,
I want to hold you again.
I feel you
By my side,
Holding me up
As I fall in love with you.

I call you,
Yet you can't hear.
You are so far away
That I can't stay.
I need you
In my life.
Far away though you are,
Together we will be.
I wish you
To accept me,
Take my hands in yours,
And hold me close.
I give you
Everything I am,
For you are my angel,
My lodestar.
I ask you
One thing only:
To give me an answer
When I say,
I love you,
I loved you,
I always did,
And I still do.
You're everything,
My life,
My love,
My self.
You steal my heart,
And I only wish
For the day
I'll hold you again.
Resting under a tree
One summer day

With you by my side,
I fell in love with you.
Now resting under a tree
One winter night
Without you by my side,
I yearn for you.
Love is when I'm with you.
You're the light
That makes my life bright.
I need you.
I will say it again,
And I await your reply.
Forevermore,
I will always love you.
To someone very special,
In whose memories I still linger,
Seeking an answer, I write,
Hoping a love will come my way.

I dedicated these poems to my love. They expressed my wishes and the earnest hope I harbored for Rose. Even after all that had occurred, this hope couldn't be abolished. It was elemental to the blossoming of my love for her, despite the distance between us. Dad had advised me to keep my emotions in check, but I naturally followed my instincts and feelings. To reject them would mean I was rejecting myself. As much as I wanted to wait for her words, I couldn't succeed on two fronts. While I was able to keep my mind on track, my heart yearned to see her again. I wanted to resolve this issue my way.

My stubbornness kept the outcome in doubt.

* * *

Near the end of the year, I began to speculate about my return to Sudan. I wanted to surprise my family, and I made arrangements with Dad to arrive earlier than expected. It was a secret, and I limited any discussion regarding this topic with Mom, Annie, and my friends.

I spent several nights envisioning my return to Sudan. I dreamed of how Dad would bring Mom and Annie to the airport to meet a VIP from PLAN. They would be surprised when the VIP was me. It would be a portrait in perfection. I would have a chance to hold Annie in my arms. I would have a chance to wipe Mom's tears away. And, of course, I would have a chance to high-five Dad for a plan well done.

Following this, I could accompany Annie to school and surprise my teachers and friends. For Rose, I planned to do something more special. I could ask Annie to catch her attention and bring her to the garden. I could walk out from behind the tree and surprise her! In my dreams, my return was an opportunity to assert my love.

I took a few of my exams ahead of time in order to return home earlier. I was excited about surprising Mom, Annie and everyone else. At that point, I had also decided to accept whatever would happen between Rose and me. Even if I failed at love, I would be satisfied to remain her friend.

A large part of me would always yearn for her and dream of our possibilities. But time could help me heal. It would hurt for a while, but that pain could be beautiful.

* * *

Much to my disappointment, I faced several delays during my return. I was held up in Frankfurt; by the time Dad and I fixed my problems, my travel route had to be reset. Mom obviously figured out the surprise and chided me for hiding it. Now, there was only one person remaining to surprise in my family. Annie still had no clue about my return.

After a stop in Egypt, I finally made it back to Sudan. I felt so happy to be at home with Mom and Dad. As I had predicted, Mom broke into tears when I emerged from the terminal; Dad held her shoulder, beaming in happiness. I rushed into the comfort of their arms. I had missed them so much. Giving them both a kiss on the cheek, I laughed while I explained the plan to Mom. Dad took my luggage, and we drove home to celebrate my return. Mom had dreamed of setting up an enormous banquet for my return, but I was satisfied with what we had.

It was typical of Mom to make last-minute arrangements; as I entered our apartment, I could smell the delicate fragrance of chocolate cake wafting from the kitchen. Settling down on the couch in the main hall, I was the happiest man in the world. Finally, I was home, and it felt great. While Dad returned to the office to finish his evening duties, Mom and I caught up on things at home. I decided to wait on the chocolate cake until I surprised Annie, but I was still hungry. Mom had cooked some rice and liver curry. I ate voraciously while she kept me company.

Things had worked out differently, but it didn't matter. This way was even better. Mom assisted me in surprising Annie. I decided to wait in her room when she returned from school that evening. Mom signaled me about her arrival from the kitchen, and I waited nervously in her room. She walked in—ignoring my presence—and put her things on her study table. I sat motionless on her bed and waited for her to notice me. On several occasions, she glanced in my direction but seemingly convinced herself that I was an illusion. It was only when I called her name that she realized I was real. She bounded into my arms and pushed me back; I had to grab the bed for support.

Mom walked in to the sight of Annie crying uncontrollably on my chest. It was a beautiful moment, and I was very happy. In the span of a year, she seemed to have grown up so much. My heart rose in elation, warmth, and pride. I held her in my arms and whispered, "I'm back—like I promised. I love you, Annie."

After we ate the cake, I spent the rest of the evening unpacking with the help of my family. I had purchased an old-school pocket watch for Dad, a purse for Mom, and a beautiful silver necklace for Annie. Mom cooked a delicious Indian dinner that night. Although I was fatigued from traveling, we spent the night watching a nice family movie in Tamil.

My journal entries took a better turn as I described my excitement at being home. It took awhile to adjust to the time difference and overcome the jet lag. I enjoyed helping Mom in the kitchen, playing board games with Dad and Annie, and watching movies together. I had arrived on a weekend and had to wait until Monday to visit KAS. I shared my plans to surprise Rose and my friends with Annie. She was eager to help, and I couldn't wait to deliver.

Before leaving for school on Monday morning, Annie and I revised our plan one final time. Due to the excitement, I hadn't been able to sleep. I spent most of the night thinking about Rose, Tina, and my friends, so I wasn't keen about an early morning surprise. Annie left at seven to catch the assembly at school, and I took a taxi to KAS at nine. I arrived during the first break of the day.

On the way to school, I listened to the song "Perfect" by Burn Season. I found it hard to believe I was heading to KAS, and the song provided a jovial atmosphere. The sun was slowly beginning its ascent, and I enjoyed seeing the new shopping centers and restaurants on my way to the school. At the gate, I talked to the guards; to my surprise, they recognized me and let me in.

Shielding my eyes from the sun, I took a good look around me. The first thing that caught my eye was the garden. It looked the same as ever, and I walked over to the tree with a smile. It hadn't been so long ago since I had stood under its shade to bid farewell to KAS. But now, I had finally returned. Closing my eyes, I let the moment sink in. A cool breeze brushed my face, and I looked up to see a sign reminiscent of the past. The leaves were swept up by the wind and fell on my shoulders. It felt like KAS was welcoming me with open arms.

The stage was set. My plan was to surprise my friends—and then my teachers. I made my way through the quad and saw Annie by the cafeteria. Waving to me, she ran over to ask if we should execute the plan. For some reason, after that moment in the garden, I decided to withdraw the plan and go with the flow. I wanted to see what would happen if I just went in for the surprise.

In the cafeteria, I saw Rose chatting with her friends. To see if she would recognize my voice, I called out to Rino. The reactions were instantaneous. Everyone in the cafeteria was absolutely shocked. To my surprise and pleasure, Rose reacted instinctively to my call, turning around to gape at my presence. As I embraced Rino, I had a clear view of her surprised and shocked face. As a crowd of friends surrounded me, I slowly made my way to her. I waved and said, "Hey!"

Rose covered her face with her hands. She looked like she was about to cry; this simple action made my heart flutter. It took her awhile to recover, and she looked as if she was going to give me a hug. I was more than happy to give her one, but I was wrong. The next moment, she left in search of Annie. I was certain she was angry that Annie hadn't informed her of my arrival.

Rose and the others eventually headed off to class. Rino had a free block period and went with me to visit my teachers. It was like a walk down memory lane; I enjoyed entertaining my friend and teachers with my adventures at university. Ms. Ramone, Mr. Wilson, Mrs. Wilson, and Ms. Lana were all intent on keeping me there for the rest of the evening, but I promised to visit KAS frequently during the next few weeks. I had made it in time for the graduation of Rino, Tina, and several of my other friends. I was disappointed to learn that Tina hadn't made it to school that day. I made sure that no one would tell her about my arrival to keep my surprise safe.

I caught up with Rose later that evening during her math class. I was relaxing in the library when I saw her class come in. My former calculus professor welcomed me as a guest for the session. The students were researching trigonometry and calculus. I passed by Rose at a computer and made small talk with my other friends. Occasionally, she would look my way, but I was too nervous to talk to her. I didn't know why, but it had been easier earlier when I had everyone around me. After all that had happened during the year, I was afraid of how she would respond and decided to keep my distance.

Rose wasn't taking any of it. She grabbed my arm as I passed by her table and pulled me down next to her. She whispered, "Hey! What is up with you? You've been here the whole time—and you just keep avoiding me. You aren't even maintaining eye contact. Don't do that."

I said, "I'm sorry, Rose. Just, you know, after all that happened, I was a little queasy about talking to you. I didn't know if you would respond well."

"Whatever! That was in the past. Doesn't justify you avoiding me now," Rose replied with a smile. She was spot-on about that. I sat with her during the class, alternating between talking and helping her with her studies. I had expected an anxious, awkward conversation, but it seemed like everything was all right.

After school, we hung out in the cafeteria. I recalled all the funny memories we had together. Rose was surprised by how I remembered such things. She was taken aback and repeatedly stated her disbelief that I was actually there with her. It felt good every time she said that. I was relieved to know that she had actually missed my company. It had been so long since we had talked. I didn't want to bring up any conversations regarding our relationship or our sparse communication during my time in Canada. I was just satisfied to see her again.

I would have given anything to just spend the rest of the evening with her, but KAS now didn't allow students to stay on campus after classes were completed. I learned from Rose that Tina's absence was due to her preparations for an AP exam the following day. Rose and I had a great evening together. I was so happy to see her again, and I felt at peace in having returned to KAS. Not a lot had changed at school. Seeing all my friends and teachers had certainly struck a chord in my heart. I was very happy.

After I returned home, I couldn't resist the urge to call Tina. Setting up the speaker phone, Annie and I had to listen to her scream in joy for a few minutes before we could speak. Tina was excited to hear about my return and asked if I could visit her at school the following day. I couldn't promise her that, but I suggested that we set up a social at Rider's Diner for the weekend—after she had successfully completed her AP exams. The outing could be a reunion as well as a celebration for the soon-to-be graduates. She accepted immediately when I told her the dinner was on me.

Wishing her luck in the exams, I related the day's events to Mom and Dad. I had set up a master plan, but I took satisfaction in knowing that things had progressed better than I had expected. Though I missed Mark, Kevin, Cindy, Hank, Rina, Rigel, Carlos, and my classmates, I was content to know they were venturing out on their own adventures around the world.

Lynn's family had moved to the United States a few months after my graduation, but I had maintained steady contact with her throughout the year. She was doing well and often suggested that I pay her a visit. I had also missed her presence today at KAS.

I had kept in touch with all my friends except Mark and Kevin. Unfortunately, I wasn't able to establish any sort of communication with them. I wondered where they were and hoped they were doing well.

* * *

I had the rest of the vacation to pick a time to talk to Rose about our issues. It had to happen soon. I wanted to find an opportunity to voice my thoughts clearly to her.

Tina, Rino, Annie, and a few of my friends met up at Rider's. It was a heck of a party. Tina and Rino were exuberant about their upcoming graduation. They were confident about their performances on the AP exams. Rino related the story of my arrival to Tina. Rose couldn't make it that night. As disappointing as that was, I still enjoyed my time with Tina; we got into an intense conversation about my plans for Rose.

I said, "You know, when I got your e-mail, I was extremely happy. But the year was rough. Believe it or not, the communication between Rose and me was sparse. She went so far as to even mention that my letter was a burden. I struggled for months with my anxiety about what to do. I was left with two choices—either move on or keep up hope. Her letter seemed to hint at mixed messages; when I got your side of the story, I was even more confused. I decided then that it was necessary for me to talk to her directly about this. I'm not sure when I'm going to do it, but I'm waiting for the opportune moment."

"That's good, bro. That's a good plan. I think it's good to keep some space and clear your thoughts. When you're ready, pop the question again. I now understand the confusion you might have experienced upon reading my e-mail. I'm sorry about that."

"It's okay, sis. I'm glad that you were at least there for me—and you kept your promise to look after Rose," I said with a smile. Despite the ruckus around us, our conversation seemed to flow on its own.

"Of course I kept my word. It's good to see that you didn't completely break down. I was worried about how you were taking things over there. E-mails and text messages are never really good enough for conveying your feelings to someone else. So I certainly approve of your decision to talk about this directly with her. But what if she says no?"

"Well, I've been trying to keep an open mind about this scenario. As of now, I'm really not expecting anything. I loved her a lot—and I still do. If she were to refute these claims, then of course I would feel hurt and misled. But I've been feeling that pain for over a year. I should be fine. I'm satisfied with being her friend. I can't deny that I would still love her, but this time I would have to do so as a friend. Life would have to go on either way, right? I can't keep denying the reality."

"Well then, if you're set on this course, that's all I wanted to know. I really wish you the best, bro. Whatever happens, I'm always here to help you out."

"Thank you, Tina. You've helped me so much over the years, and I'm indebted to you. We'll see where life takes me. It felt magical to visit KAS again. Spending that evening with Rose was awesome, and I enjoyed my time with her. Even if I were to fail in my love, I want to succeed in our friendship. That's where it all started, and if we are going to end on these terms, I won't be disappointed. At least we'll both know where we stand with each other. That's what matters to me right now. Time will take care of things afterward. Now, enough of this, tonight's your night! Let's make a toast for the soon-to-be graduates!" I said vehemently, putting an end to our conversation and receiving raucous applause from our friends.

I enjoyed my time with Rino, Tina, and the others on that night. At the end of May, I went to the graduation. The ceremony brought back memories of my own graduation. I congratulated Rino, Tina, and their classmates.

Their adventures in life were yet to begin, and I was sure that they would do well wherever they went. Rino left a few days after the graduation. He was returning to pursue his higher studies in India. We promised to keep in touch and had one last meeting before his departure. I was able to convey my pleasure at being granted his friendship. I was going to miss my friend, but I knew that—even if we didn't get a chance to see each other again—we would always have our memories from KAS.

A few weeks later, I received news from Lynn. She had just graduated from high school in the United States. She had been accepted to Georgetown University. She planned to major in International Studies. I was happy to hear from her, and I wished her well in her endeavors.

Graduation brought down the number of friends I knew at KAS. Several of the students who graduated left the country within a few weeks. It was reminiscent of my own journey a year earlier. Tina's parents had decided that she would enroll in one of the universities in Sudan. For now, they had made preparations for a visit home to Sweden.

Mr. Wilson, Mrs. Wilson, and Ms. Ramone told me about the end of their teaching contracts at KAS. Mr. and Mrs. Wilson were traveling during their vacation and would begin new teaching positions at an international school in Nepal. Ms. Ramone had decided to retire and was returning to the United States with her family. Her son was set to begin his studies at Virginia Tech. Ms. Lana planned to return to the Philippines to enjoy a vacation with her family.

On the night of graduation, I thanked each of my teachers for all the help, inspiration, and assistance they had provided me during my years at KAS. I would return to Canada in August, and I knew there would not be a chance to see them again. They had made the best of my four years at this school, and I owed them a lot.

Mr. Wilson's inspiration had helped me pursue my degree in astrophysics. Mrs. Wilson's motivation had taken me to greater heights in the arts. Ms. Ramone and Ms. Lana had served as good mentors in the social and academic landscapes. Their counsel had been valuable to me on many occasions. I had wonderful memories of all four of my teachers. I promised to keep in touch with all of them.

The departure of such personalities meant the end of an era at KAS. My legacy at KAS had been built upon my relationships with them. I felt melancholic that it was time for a new beginning. Rose and a few others were the only connections I would have left at KAS in the following year. Truly, it seemed like the end of a fairy tale.

* * *

The days passed by quickly. After the departure of my friends and teachers, I spent most of my time with my family at home. We wanted to make the most of our moments together even if it were in simple activities such as cooking or watching movies. Even these ordinary days would serve as great memories for my upcoming departure. Dad's contract in Sudan would end in September, and my family would move to Sierra Leone. We had several invitations from family friends and colleagues from Dad's organization for dinners, hangouts, and trips around Sudan.

Although I was busy at home, I tried my best to set up social events with my remaining friends. This mainly included Tina and Rose. As we neared mid-July and Tina's departure to Sweden, I decided that it would be an opportune moment to discuss things with Rose. Tina and Annie were telling me to get an answer as soon as possible. Tina invited us to her home on the night before her departure. Rose and a few other friends joined us. The small congregation would allow me to easily find the space and opportunity to chat with Rose without any disruptions.

On the way to Tina's house, I revealed my plans to Annie. I needed her assistance in diverting Rose's attention. Annie was eager to help; once we arrived she informed Tina that I would be making my move that night. I felt exhilarated. The night could prove to be the stepping-stone toward something new. My fate lay in Rose's answer. I had been waiting so long and was wondering about what would happen that night.

We arrived at Tina's house at eight o'clock. People began filing in, and soon the living room was occupied. Within a few minutes of her arrival, Rose informed us that she had to leave at 9:30. Her parents were keeping her on a strict curfew. I didn't want to miss my chance; while the others engaged in conversations, Annie prodded me to make a move. With the help of Tina's sister, she was able to indirectly clear the crowd. While they took a trip around the house, I had an opportunity to speak to Rose.

I had butterflies in my stomach as I approached her. I had a weird feeling that this was the end—a feeling that it wasn't going to happen—but I couldn't resolve this by myself. I needed to talk to her. I needed to hear it from her. Walking over to her side, I bent down and whispered, "Hey? Can we talk?"

Rose nodded, and we found a spot by the couches in the main hall. We sat on opposite sides of a table. After a few minutes of silence, our conversation began.

Rose started by asking what I had wanted to talk about. I didn't hesitate and apologized for everything that had come to pass between us: the letter, my selfishness, the burdens I had placed on her, and how I appreciated that she was grateful enough to still consider me a friend. I told her she was a great person and how this experience had made me realize my selfishness.

She said, "Everyone is selfish in love. There is no denying that."

"Rose, I'm an idiot. But let me ask you one last time. After all the memorable moments we have shared together and the personal messages we have sent to each other, in the end—after all of this— all you ever felt for me was friendship?"

Rose's response confirmed my fears. She nodded and said, "Yes. I had been over this for quite some time. Your letter was a bit of a burden. You were going everywhere with it—so repetitively. I've never seen you stammer like that in any of your writing—not to mention all the poems and gifts you left behind. It was too much." She refused to look at me while she talked.

I knew that asking her again was hurting her. I wanted to know more, but she had said enough. Her answer was resolute, and I knew that I couldn't persist with these questions. I could feel my soul crashing down. I couldn't keep it up any longer. With pain coursing through my heart, I said, "Tear up the letter. I hope you did. I don't want to be a burden on you anymore. I'm sorry. I was afraid of this. It was one of the reasons that I couldn't approach you on the day I returned to KAS. I was afraid of how you would respond to my presence after all this happened."

"That's where you don't know me well. What were you afraid of? That we couldn't be friends? Nope, you saw me pull you down and make you sit next to me that evening. You enjoyed your time in my company—and I felt the same way. I was happy to see you again. Despite all that has happened, we are still friends—and we will only and always be friends."

Those last few words stung, but I knew I couldn't refute them. My mind was finding it difficult to absorb the reality that was unfolding before my eyes, but I forced myself to take the initiative and ask the question. I said, "So, is there another guy? Do you have someone else you like?"

"Yes. I loved—and still love—this one person from my past. It's been a few years, but my feelings have remained strong."

She remained silent after saying these words. Her silence resonated with her strong feelings for this person.

"Does he know that you like him?"

"I know that he does. Circumstances set us apart, but I still hope to reunite with him."

"So you think about him a lot?" I said. I wanted a complete answer.

"No, it's not like that. It's been years since we last saw each other, but he was my first love. It was an experience beyond any other. I moved on with my life when I came to Sudan. I had a few relationships, but he was always on my mind. He was my first love. I'm sure you understand."

The irony of her words struck me with great intensity. When she had mentioned her first love, I had instinctively reacted. I wanted to say, "You were my first love!" But I remained silent and thrust those words deep into the chasms of my heart where they were locked away. I had promised not to be a burden on her anymore; my words wouldn't make that any easier.

Struggling with my emotions and a broken heart, I said, "I hope you are able to find him again. Keep up your hope. I realized a long time ago that the farther you are from someone, the more you tend to realize how important they are to you. Sometimes the distance serves to strengthen our bonds with another person—be it in love or friendship. It is up to us to persevere and keep strong. I know that you can do it, and I wish you the best. My last request for the night is that you throw away the letter I gave you."

"Thanks for understanding, but I don't plan on throwing away the letter. It's funny. At first, I was surprised when I read it, but sometimes when I look back at the writing, I laugh. I don't know. It can remain as a memory."

Her words hurt. I knew that she hadn't meant to offend me, and I had to accept the inevitable reality that I could only be her friend. Nothing was going to change that. Throughout the conversation, I had envisioned myself sitting next to her and holding her. Even though a distance remained in reality, I dreamed of her sitting beside me.

After a few minutes, we regrouped with the others. Annie and Tina looked up to me expectantly. I responded with a smile. The truth had finally been revealed. It was time to move on. Rose's father picked her up at 9:30. Annie and I left a few minutes later. I congratulated Tina again on her graduation and wished her well in her studies. I would be long gone before her return; this was our final farewell. I was going to miss her so much. Annie and I took a taxi back home. Tina's house was half an hour away from our apartment. During this time, I told her everything about my discussion with Rose. Annie could sense the pain in my voice. It was difficult to describe the details, but I gave her a general idea. My mind was reeling from what had happened. It felt as if I had left my heart behind during the conversation with Rose.

Tina sent Annie a text message about the results. Under my instructions, Annie replied, "They're just friends. Rose doesn't feel that way at all. Bro is doing okay. He will be okay. Says he will keep in touch. Love you from the both of us. Take care, Tina."

It seemed as if I had been right about it for so long. The flicker of hope in my heart was the cause of my pain. The fact that I somehow knew this was going to happen made me feel worse. I was silent for the rest of the ride.

I recalled my memories of Rose. Just as with Rigel, I wanted to know what had gone through Rose's mind when she replied to me that night. I found comfort in knowing that we could still be friends. I would have to bury this love deep in my heart to have a normal conversation with her again—without letting my feelings get the better of me. I needed time to heal.

When we got home, I wrote a farewell letter to Tina. Writing about what had happened and relating the experience to Tina gave me a sense of relief. My life had revolved around this question for over a year. As much as it hurt to find the answer, I felt as if a weight had been lifted from my chest. I didn't know if that was good or bad. Mom and Dad suspected that something had happened, but I needed some time for myself. I wanted to sort it out on my own. I was glad that they were okay with that.

Annie kept me company. I wanted her to be with me. We spent our time listening to romantic songs and singing along. Even then, the events of the night replayed in my mind. Eventually I couldn't take it anymore. I retreated to my room for the night. I thought about everything that had come to pass in the span of a few years. I wondered if Rose had felt anything when we talked. It hurt me more than anything to know that she had never felt any notion of love for me—throughout all these months, days, hours, minutes, and seconds. Not even once.

My heart still sought to be with her, but I knew I could only dream of such a thing. It was nothing else but an illusion—a one-sided love. That was all. I hoped that whoever she was waiting for knew her worth. I hoped whoever was lucky enough to gain her love truly deserved her. Tears rolled down my cheeks, and I clutched my heart in pain and sorrow. I wanted to cry out, but I didn't.

Despite what had happened, I realized my love had always been true. It was an unrequited love—but it was a great experience. The reality of this experience could never be changed, but how I perceived these events could be. As sleep took me away, I realized that this experience would be with me forever. I couldn't change that for the world, but I could always try to start anew.

* * *

Love happened to me, and I was desperate to keep it till the end. Maybe that was my mistake. I dreamed with a broken heart that night, but I also thanked Rose for everything. I would always remember her.

After Tina's departure, I wondered how to move on from this experience. The weeks passed swiftly. Spending time with my family helped suppress the pain and heal my broken heart. In the company of their love, I felt rejuvenated.

My days in Sudan were also coming to an end. If I had any intention of seeing my family after my second year of studies, I would be visiting them in Sierra Leone. This was officially my final stay in Sudan. I vowed to return to Khartoum one day.

I didn't get a chance to see Rose before my departure, but I sent her a note to thank her for everything. I realized how distant my love had been. My love for her had nurtured in the distance between us. Even after all our time together, I had never come close to holding her. I had wished for many things in the recesses of my heart, but they had never happened.

What I had felt for Rose was beautiful, and I couldn't deny it. I had once dreamed of holding her hand. I had dreamed of many things in my love for her. Yet, in the end, everything had been a dream. I was finally able to discern the difference, but the dream had been beautiful while it lasted. I knew it would always take me back to a part of my life I could never forget.

I spent my last days in Khartoum with my family. Another separation was on the horizon, but we were happy. Our memories kept us strong, and we looked forward to a reunion in the near future. On August 17, 2010, I left Sudan to continue my studies at the University of Alberta.

A year earlier, I had embarked on this same journey with a heavy heart and a hesitant mind. From the day I was born till the day I die, I intend to believe that life will always provide an answer. This time, it seemed to hint at a new beginning, a new chapter in my life. I smiled at this realization and, eager to get started, ventured forth to my future.

* * *

In life, there are no endings. There are only new beginnings—and that's what happened to me over the next few years. I have now completed my final year of studies at the University of Alberta. I'm not sure where I will go after convocation, but I take pleasure in the uncertainty.

Life granted me several lessons over the past few years. I even got a few surprises. I still keep in touch with my friends and receive updates from them. Ms. Lana and I have plans to meet up. I think I could save our meeting for a visit to Sudan. She frequently posts new albums on Facebook that detail the changes at KAS. I'm happy that she is doing well. Mr. and Mrs. Wilson are still in Nepal, and Ms. Ramone has settled in America with her family. I've talked to Dad about taking a break after university for a year; I want to enjoy life and maybe take some trips to visit my friends and teachers. I think that would be a sweet deal.

In my third year of undergraduate studies, I was able to contact Mark and Kevin. We had a heart-to-heart conversation. I was especially happy to hear that they had pursued their academic interests. Mark was on his way for a degree in evolutionary psychology, and Kevin was pursuing medical studies. The past was behind us, and we renewed our friendship. Mark is currently in Toronto, and he expects a visit from me in the near future. Kevin has settled in Sudan with his family, and I intend to meet up with him when I return to Khartoum. Aside from my two best friends, I also welcomed Rose to the University of Alberta that year.

When Rose decided to attend the University of Alberta, I was happy to receive her. It had only taken a moment to fall in love with her, but it took years to accept the circumstances of our friendship. When I met up with her during orientation, I realized I had moved on. Rose had felt nothing but friendship with me. There was nothing but love in what I felt for her. Love and friendship are two different things, but they share the same emotions.

During our time together in Edmonton, I realized that my love for Rose had not failed. It had succeeded. I was finally able to comprehend Rose's true identity and accept her as a friend. My unrequited love for Rose taught me the truth about friendship. I found the love she held for me as a friend. She had shared the truth with me, but I had misread it. That was the gift I had been waiting for. I finally saw the deeper meaning of it all.

We have interacted several times in Edmonton. We even took some classes together. I'm happy to be able to communicate with her on the basis of these truths. In this way, I can say that our last summer was truly beautiful. She is a good friend, and I am happy about the moments we share. I wrote a poem inspired by my friendship for Rose and the Tamil movie *Vinnaithandi Varuvaya*.

The movie chronicled a story parallel to what has occurred between Rose and me. *Vinnaithandi Varuvaya* means, "Will you cross the skies for me?" The poem is a tribute to the wonderful journey of our friendship.

For You, I Will Cross the Skies

It all began one day
When love came into my way.
One moment was all that was needed,
A love that was unheeded.
I fell for her then,
Not knowing where or when.
I followed her in my mind;

In my heart, she was mine.
So many things happened,
Leaving some feelings unquestioned.
I fell in love with her,
And she drove me to tears.
A love I confessed,
A friendship she desired.
In a thousand tears of my own,
We departed in an end that came soon.
The uncertainty remained,
Her memories unrestrained.
My heart still sought
The love that it had long lost.
A year went by;
In silence I lay.
Then I saw her that day,
And it all came back again.
Being so far,
I still loved her.
So many dreams that had come by,
I wanted to have her by my side.
To have her in my arms,
To hold her forever.
Her smile reminiscent,
Her touch unforgotten.
Yet,
The question still remained.
In my heart,
I felt I knew the answer.
A love I confessed,
A friendship she desired.
Things passed by;
Life went on.
And a story I wrote

For a love that I fought.
The memories will be;
They will always stay with me.
The question has always been there,
But our love had come through.
Beautiful was she,
The question, "Will you cross the skies for me?"
What we had for each other,
Something I will hold dear.
She came into my life,
But it was never meant to be.
A heart I held for her,
A heart that I still hold.
Our times wouldn't be forgotten;
This love would not be gone.
Our consequences,
She was all I ever wanted.
Two hearts,
One loving soul.
I liked this pain.
And a love it became.
What we had was beautiful,
And it will be with us.
Together. Forever.
In our last summer.
Without tears, I write what's in my heart,
A love that I had always sought,
A love that I have not lost.
Knowing our memories will be
Makes me say once again,
Like on that day,
"For you, I will cross the skies."

My love for Rose was unrequited and as such was never complete. Its completion was found only in our friendship. I still hadn't found true love.

It isn't true love unless it is reciprocated and accepted by a rightful other. True love assumes no expectations, bringing two people together, dictated by nothing more than their acceptance of each other's feelings and lives.

By the end of my third year of studies, I was still hopeful for a wonderful, new adventure in my life. True love still beckoned me, and I knew somewhere out there the right person was waiting for me. I was hopeful of it. I mentioned this to Dad and he applauded me. He said, "Now, my son, you have learned to control the outcome."

Since then, my life has taken a new turn. I have my own family of friends in Edmonton, and I've thoroughly enjoyed the enriching experience of university. Mom, Dad, and Annie are currently in Sierra Leone. As a family, we've faced several obstacles. Their support, counsel, and love have helped me succeed at university and pull through in life. I love them so much, and I can't thank them enough for what they have given me. I think that, after these four years, we can finally settle down, sit back, and enjoy our time together as a family.

* * *

Life—it is a consummate experience. It takes one away in a tide of feelings: passion, grief, happiness, and isolation … Feelings make us human. They bind us to the mortal plane; we all share these feelings. It isn't easy to find someone to love and care for—someone who loves you back with no bounds. True love and friendship can exist for a moment, but their memories last forever.

One is never born alone. Someday—in some way—we find true friends and family. We learn to live beside them and are willing to sacrifice anything—even ourselves—for them. Life is about smiling against the toughest of odds. One should never give up—no matter what—to overcome pain and become stronger. Despite all our ups and downs, one can always make a hell of a story about it. At the end of the day we are all human, and one can never deviate from being human.

Everyone should cherish family, friendship, and love. Even if you aren't related to someone, that person may still be your friend, brother, sister, father, or mother. There's no questioning involved— you just know it. Most importantly, you're never too old to follow your dreams, whatever they are, because dreams are eternal.

Life happens on its own accord. That's how it's always been for me. After all these years, I've come to understand this. If I remain still and hold on to my past, nothing will ever change. The memories would linger forever. But if I take a single step forward with a smile and a refreshed hope, I have a feeling that something will change— and something good will happen.

I've stumbled and fumbled my way to where I am now. But sometimes, that's what life is all about. Though it has its share of struggles, I've learned to face my challenges with a smile. Everything has its time and place. I treasure what I have now: the love of my family, the wonderful memories of high school, friends, and the everlasting horizon of a new adventure, which allowed me to find my first true love in another, with someone who accepted my heart as I did hers, and who I now cherish.

The experience was beyond any other and showed me the difference in having someone who reciprocated my love and accepted me for who I am. Sometimes even the most ordinary of life's circumstances are beautiful, and that was how it was for me with her in our first meeting. Aside from my family, I had never experienced such a bond with another. It is something that I now strive hard to protect and keep close.

Does fate or destiny play a role in our lives? In my case, I'd rather not think about it at all. For me, I'm happy with where I am in my life. To have a bright future along with a wonderful family, amazing friends, and now a beautiful love to indulge in, I couldn't ask for more. Maybe life isn't about seeking things, but rather letting it come to you, and learning to recognize the opportunities when they are there. Despite the broad expanse of time that lies ahead in my life, and the uncertainties of the future, the support of my family and my love prompts me to believe that, at the end of the day, everything's going to be all right.

This memoir will always be a reminder and tribute to the token of friendship, love, and familial ties with everyone who has influenced my life. Gathering all our dreams, memories, wishes, and happiness, I intend to head for the future, to a new place where I'm sure that one day, we'll all meet again.

Everyone, thank you for everything. Because of you, our last summer came to be.